RUGBY
WORLD CUP
2003

RUGBY WORLD CUP 2003

Rugby World Cup 2003 ñ The Official Souvenir Book was produced by News Custom Publishing.

Level 4, HWT Tower
40 City Rd
Southbank, Victoria
Australia 3006
Tel: 61 3 9292 2000

ISBN 1-876176-36-9

Publisher James Weston

EDITORIAL
Managing Editor Matthew Clayton
RWC 2003 Editor Finn Bradshaw
Art Director Randall Smith
Contributing Editor Stuart Sykes
Chief Sub-Editor Martyn Haynes
Editorial contributors
Ian Borthwick (*L'Equipe*, Paris)
Mick Cleary (*The Telegraph*, London)
Andy Colquhoun (*MWP*, Cape Town)
Jon Geddes (*The Daily Telegraph*, Sydney)
Peter Jenkins (*The Daily Telegraph*, Sydney)
Stephen Jones (*The Sunday Times*, London)
Duncan Johnstone (*Sportscast*, Auckland)
Bruce Wilson (*News Limited*, London)

ART
Designer Ken Leung
Photography Getty Images, HWT Library

PRODUCTION
Office Manager Jenine Tinker
Circulation Manager Margaret Lemac
Editorial Production Manager Michael Brown
Print Manager John Batten
Production Co-ordinator Cathy Murray
Quality Control/Imaging Manager Graham Patrick
Colour Separations HWT Imaging
Printing Butler and Tanner Ltd, Frome and London

RUGBY
WORLD CUP
2003

THE OFFICIAL SOUVENIR BOOK

NEWS
CUSTOM
PUBLISHING

Contents

10   **RWC 2003 captured:** Australia welcomes the world

20   **A tournament retrospective:** RWC 2003 review

28   **IRB Heineken Player of the Year**

34   **Turning points:** The tournament's defining moments

44   **Pool A review**

52   **Pool B review**

60   **Pool C review**

68   **Pool D review**

82   **The quarter-finals**

94   **Last four: the semi-finals**

108   **Third-place playoff**

114   **The final**

126   **Through the lens:**
Essential images of the tournament

136   **Team of the tournament:**
The cream of the crop from RWC 2003

156   **Match synopses and statistics**

174   **RWC 2003 by the numbers:** A statistical overview

178   **The last word**

Celebrate good times: Uruguay's captain
Diego Aguirre hoists Juan Menchaca in the
air as they celebrate their team's victory over
Georgia at Aussie Stadium in Sydney.

A host of reasons to celebrate

By any standards, Rugby World Cup 2003 has been a massive success. Targets have been reached and surpassed in all areas. The crowds have been larger, the global audience bigger and the income generated greater than ever before.

But much more than that, rugby has reached the hearts and minds of men and women, boys and girls, not only throughout a host country which so enthusiastically and warmly embraced the event, the teams, the players and the legion of supporters, but in so many other parts of the world where the game has no history or tradition.

The friendship generated by the tournament the length and breadth of Australia, fuelled by the hospitality and superb organisation of the hosts, has been a joy to behold. What other sport can so comfortably balance the intensity of the contest on the field with the fellowship off it?

And the rugby public has been royally entertained. There have been compelling matches and breathtaking action; we have seen courage, sportsmanship, supreme athleticism and sublime individual skill, and for all 20 participating teams and their players, there has been the unforgettable experience of having taken part in the world's premier rugby event. Roll on 2007.

Syd Millar

DR SYD MILLAR
CHAIRMAN
RUGBY WORLD CUP AND INTERNATIONAL RUGBY BOARD

RUGBY WORLD CUP 2003 CAPTURED

One world in union: Rugby adds its own unmistakable symbol to the twin icons of Sydney's cityscape – the Opera House and the Harbour Bridge. Few sports build bridges between nations as well as rugby union's greatest tournament does, as the game's great powers share the limelight with new players on the stage. In the pages that follow, four quintessential images sum up the colour, excitement and, above all, the spirit of Rugby World Cup 2003.

On the opening night of Rugby
World Cup 2003, Sydney puts
on its finest face to greet the
20 competing nations.
Few places on Earth know
how to celebrate a special
occasion better than the
Harbour City – and what better
occasion than the game they
play in Heaven?

Pacific islands, war-like stance: Tonga's players perform their nation's ritual warrior challenge. The colourful Tongans, led by the irrepressible Pierre Hola, brought their own brand of running rugby to Australia and carried the fight to some of the game's most powerful nations.

12

Focus on the flag: Japan was a joy to follow, winning friends galore in Townsville in particular with its fans' passionate support for the game and its rising sons. They may not have influenced the outcome of Rugby World Cup 2003, but they certainly left their mark.

Pointing in the right direction: Samoa, and its scrum-half Steven So'oialo, may not have made it through to the quarter-finals of RWC 2003, but 18 tries and an open style made the islanders some of the most popular players of the tournament. Finishing third in Pool C behind giants like England and South Africa was no disgrace.

Spirit of the game: Building bridges is the object of the exercise, even after a tough encounter on a rain-soaked battlefield in Sydney. Swapping jerseys and handshakes means the players of Ireland and Namibia part as friends – until their next meeting.

Six weeks of celebration

The greatest Rugby World Cup, beyond any doubt. In fact, comparisons are a waste of time, because in 2003 Australia simply re-wrote the rule book for staging rugby's six weeks of glory. There was barely a single aspect which did not come through triumphantly, and the sense of anticlimax when the world departed Australia in the days after the final was palpable.

Perhaps Australia's joy was diminished by the fact that the Webb Ellis Cup went north for the first time, taken home in the giant hands of Martin Johnson, the England captain, who is now, beyond doubt, the most important figure of this era in the world game. But if it is possible for Aussies to take a broader view when it comes to calamity at the hands of the old country, they may well find compensations.

Australia (the Union, the country and the people) staged everything quite magnificently, not only sending the profile and future prospects of the union code soaring throughout the country, but contributing significantly to a new era of boom and prosperity throughout the world game. Set against the inconvenience of a last-gasp drop goal by a phenomenon called Jonny Wilkinson, these achievements are weighty.

Australia opened its heart. Attendances at the matches were so high that they staggered even the optimists, with over 20,000 turning out in Perth on a wet Sunday to see Georgia play Samoa, and almost a capacity crowd drawn to Aussie Stadium, Sydney, for the match between Georgia and Uruguay. But these are just examples – Australia's people had quite obviously decided that they were going to join in the party, and they turned up festooned in all kinds of face-paint, costumes, national favours and general vividness.

They also turned up armed with a traditional generosity, adopting the smaller teams on a local basis. All those present, including the two teams and the spectators, will always speak with something approaching awe of the match staged in Launceston, Tasmania, between Namibia and Romania. In a brilliantly simple marketing ploy, so typical of an ingenuity demonstrated throughout

BELOW National pride in evidence as the Romanian players celebrate their victory over Namibia in Launceston.

OPPOSITE No dampening these spirits: the rugby world has come to Australia and the show is on!

the six weeks of the tournament, Tasmanians were asked to support one team if they had been born in an odd year, and the other team if they had been born in an even year.

The monumental attendance figures continued throughout and the general passions and warmth reached a natural conclusion at Telstra Stadium for the final. The atmosphere was sensational, the respective groups of spectators bitingly partisan, but there was a humour and a grasp of reality just below the surface which ensured that the whole occasion ended with sportsmanship and sporting balance.

The basis of this fine Australian legacy to the future of the Rugby World Cup was the fact that it was played in Australia alone. As we look toward RWC 2007, the advantages of a sole host are all the more obvious. Any other conclusion would be ridiculous, because the whole festival of rugby in 2003 was based on one population's love for one country, and their absolute determination to show that pride and focus before the eyes and the television cameras of the world.

On the playing field, it is now the Southern Hemisphere teams which must look to change and improve. When every team was on its best form, then the top European teams compared more than favourably. South Africa was not the force it has

been in previous tournaments, losing to New Zealand in an anti-climactic quarter-final match in Melbourne.

New Zealand showed devastating form in its pool matches, but there was always the suspicion that it did not have forwards of sufficient power and merit to get past the other top contenders. This suspicion was borne out in spades as a passionate, powerful and clever Australia dumped the All Blacks in the semi-final.

The other semi-final pitted the two champs of Europe, England and France. England had only coasted through the early matches in the tournament, then had trouble fending off a delightful Welsh effort in a quarter-final at Suncorp Stadium, Brisbane – now a quite magnificent arena. Yet if England was not

deliberately fooling people, then quite obviously it was holding things in reserve, beating France to power into the final.

Earlier, the event had been galvanised by two matches involving Wales. The Welsh had been patchy in their pool games, but they played an amazing part in the final pool game against New Zealand, arguably the most thrilling contest of the whole event. Wales actually led into the final quarter and played with a wit and pace which it maintained splendidly, albeit in defeat, in its quarter-final against England.

As the final approached and with most of the other teams departed for home, spectators and rugby followers could reflect on a rich tournament. Teams like Romania, Uruguay, Japan, Georgia and Fiji, all of them with less resources

than the larger nations, showed real elan. Fiji played marvellously in a narrow and probably undeserved defeat against Scotland, while Samoa put up a tremendous fight against England in Melbourne.

Furthermore, even though Italy was effectively the first team to be knocked out, it did reveal a fine hand of new young talent.

The tournament threw up more individual heroes and more individual dazzle than any previous RWC. Italy contributed well, especially with the richly-promising young No.8, Sergio Parisse. Romania, improving after years in world rugby's nether regions, showed a refreshing

ABOVE Catch 'em young, and never mind what language they speak! The smile on this young lady's face says all we need to know about the atmosphere at RWC 2003.

OPPOSITE One world in union as the players of South Africa and Samoa offer thanks together following their match at Suncorp Stadium.

OPPOSITE BOTTOM The signs are good as England's Iain Balshaw celebrates scoring for the eventual World Champions against Samoa.

morale and resistance and in no one was this better personified than in that flanker of extraordinary courage, Ovidiu Tonita. Fiji had a sensational attacking player in the dazzling Rupeni Caucau, who scored an extraordinary try against France before he almost roasted Scotland with two more.

Georgia, a nation which apparently owns just one scrummaging machine, managed to turn out a forward pack of convincing power, based on some formidable front-on props; Argentina, compelling to watch for the excellence of its play on a narrow front and inspired by Gus Pichot at scrum-half, came within an ace of dumping Ireland. Yet there

was no team which did not contribute individuals of significance.

Ultimately, the leading tournament heroes were always going to come from the top teams and by the end, the Wilkinson phenomenon had approached in size and significance the one surrounding Jonah Lomu in South Africa in 1995. Wilkinson may be, pound for pound, the greatest tackler the game has seen, but he lacks Lomu's terrifying power and immediacy.

Nevertheless, the sheer consistent brilliance of his kicking and his all-round game forked lightning throughout Australia. Long before the end, his gang of minders grew and grew. As Martin Johnson admitted, there is no rugby player ever born he would prefer to have had behind him as the England pack delivered the ball for the final drop kick in the last 20 seconds of the second period of extra time in the final.

It was an occasion which threatened to stop the heart, such were the twists and turns. Frankly, England really should have had things sewn up long before the end of normal time, but meandered tactically. This left it open to late Australian

revivals, confirmed with an equalising penalty from Elton Flatley with the last kick of normal time, and another from Flatley only a couple of minutes before the end of extra time. It was only after this one that England drove on and Wilkinson kicked the golden goal.

There was a welcome grace from the two camps after the match, with Eddie Jones, the Australian coach, and George Gregan holding up their hands and declaring that the English were deserved winners, that they played good rugby and that justice was done. This was in contrast to some

of the sniping which occurred in the media between some of the big games, but the truth was that the coaches and other hierarchy members tended to act as adults, which polished the image of the event to a gloss.

What of the host nation? Obviously, they were devastated not to be able to defend their title in front of their own public. But there was a sense that this is a team still growing, a team which could well find itself in a year or two and mount a strong challenge in France in 2007. Players such as Matt Giteau, Stirling Mortlock and Lote Tuqiri

ABOVE A time for sad farewells too: Ireland captain Keith Wood and his French counterpart Fabien Galthié ring down the curtain on their wonderful careers.

OPPOSITE So long, see you next time! Canada's players, like so many from rugby's smaller nations, took huge pleasure in flying the flag and being part of the family at RWC 2003.

gave Australia cutting edges and once their plans to develop a more powerful forward base come to fruition, then the world may well find that Australia's slight dip in 2003 proves to be temporary.

Certainly, they have every incentive: the England front row of Trevor Woodman, Steve Thompson and Phil Vickery, which dominated the Wallabies in the final, is young enough to stay on en bloc for France 2007. Yet in terms of the excellence of the players, there were other factors to consider. Perhaps those of us involved in rugby take for granted the good behaviour and decorum of the top players.

This was some of the most pressurised sporting action seen in the world all year. But Rugby World Cup 2003 saw not one single positive drug test. It saw not one single outburst of real viciousness, it saw no sustained enmities carried on after matches. It also saw no extraneous activity in the form of bad behaviour off the field.

After Australia's demonstration as hosts, the sky is the limit for this wonderful tournament. England, quite beautifully prepared by Clive Woodward and his team, lasting stronger than anyone despite their rather ageing squad, were conclusive winners. But there was satisfaction of sorts for most of the other teams. And there was a magnificent triumph for the hosts. They showed the world how to run a festival, a party, a cultural exchange, a political forum and a world-class sporting event, and all done concurrently in six extraordinary weeks.

Jonny be good – and he was

England expected, and Jonny Wilkinson delivered. His steel-nerved drop goal in the final minute of extra time in the final capped a glorious RWC 2003 for the tournament's top scorer. Jonny Wilkinson is a perfectionist: his all-round skills were almost the perfect contribution to his country's Cup-winning campaign.

The trains from Telstra Stadium back into Sydney were rocking, and there was one song that dominated the party: catchy, easy to remember, music to English ears, discord to Australian. It goes: "Ohhh, Jonny Jonny, Jonny Jonny Jonny Jonny Wil-kin-son." Repeat ad infinitum, ad nauseam.

Still, you could hardly blame the English fans for their euphoria. As was pointed out often enough, it had been a long time between drinks. England were seen as serial underachievers in all four previous RWCs and there had been no gold in the trophy cabinet since 1966 and all that. What harm, then, in a little ditty dedicated to the man whose dropped goal in the final seconds had sent the fans on their delirious way?

Wilkinson already had been named the player of the year in a poll of his rugby-playing peers before kick-off. The night after England's triumph his position as the world's best was confirmed at the IRB dinner in a separate poll of distinguished experts. Because of that one, right-footed, wrong-footed dropped goal, it was England that was named team of the year. Only the most churlish of losers could begrudge either title.

The England fly-half topped the RWC 2003 scoring table with 113 points without even playing in the 111-13 defeat of Uruguay when he might

have expected to add another bagful of points. In that tally, though, he did not score a single try and some might speculate that indicated Wilkinson was a one-trick pony. That would be to underestimate this remarkable player.

Go back to the final. There have been few Test matches played with such an intensity of defence as England and Australia laid on in those memorable 100 minutes. Wilkinson was always in the thick of that, one tackle against Matt Giteau so bone-crushingly head-on that it left Giteau winded and Wilkinson himself prone and apparently semi-conscious. It was a heart-stopping moment for Clive Woodward and all England, but this 24-year-old is no softie who kicks. He was soon back on his feet, and his was the key extra pair of hands that set up Jason Robinson's try.

He had already come from scoring all 24 of England's points against France in a match that led to the hysterical outbursts and frothy-mouthed accusations of "bor-ing bor-ing bor-ing" against England and Wilkinson in almost all sections of the Australian media – a charge, interestingly, not repeated in France, Wilkinson's victim.

More level heads noted that Wilkinson had operated beautifully behind an ordered and disciplined England pack that steadily wore France

OPPOSITE Grace under pressure: Wilkinson carried the expectations of a nation into RWC 2003 but stayed cool, calm, and collected most of England's points to cap an outstanding year.

LEFT Classic Wilko: this is the familiar pose that has made Jonny Wilkinson an international star and the driving force behind his country's run of success.

OPPOSITE Wilkinson, his kicking and his all-round game came into ever-sharper focus as RWC 2003 went on.

out of the semi-final. Of course he was cocooned by his back row; that is what back-rowers are there to do. He kicked three of the sweetest imaginable dropped goals in frightful conditions, the rain sweeping across the stadium in sheets. Before the match the French press was worrying that six men could win the match – England's front five plus Wilkinson – and they got that right.

Who recalls now, though, that before France there were serious doubts being expressed about Goldenboots, King Jonny, Supershot – call him what you will? It was not just in the Australian media, either; back home people were wondering after England's near-run thing against Wales if perhaps too much was being asked of one man. His kicking momentarily faltered, and he seemed leaden-footed and uninspired in attack. The Welsh rattled him so much that Mike Catt was brought on as cover, and to kick from hand.

In the week between Wales in Brisbane and France in Sydney, coach Clive Woodward was consistently on the back foot parrying questions about his match-winning fly-half, almost as if

Wilkinson had not scored 23 of the points in the ultimate scoreline against Wales of 28-17.

The accusations of terminal boredom were based on what is really a rugby union fallacy expressed generally by those whose allegiance is to the other rugby code: that tries are all that matter. Wilkinson was painted to represent an England incapable of try-scoring, with Wales outscoring them two-to-one and France one-to-zip in that department.

The very presence in the England side of Jonny Wilkinson had people calling for the devaluing of the dropped goal. Sydney's *Daily Telegraph* prankishly manufactured a T-shirt with a "Stop Jonny" road sign across it. Once it was clear Australia was to be the opponent in the final, the "Stop Jonny" movement became almost a cult.

It is fair to say that no single player has so dominated a Rugby World Cup, not even David Campese in his golden year of 1991. Wilkinson's presence at RWC 2003 was like Pele's when he played his World Cups. Wilkinson seemed to get about five times the exposure of anyone else.

Apart from the jaunt against Georgia, Wilkinson announced himself and his intention with 20 points out of 25 against South Africa in Perth, including – of course – two dropped goals.

This was England's first serious challenge, a tense if error-strewn affair in which Wilkinson led a backline defence that stopped South Africa from scoring a try.

The first serious doubts about England came against the worthy and brave Samoans who ran

ABOVE Who said all he
could do was kick? Wilkinson
launches himself into a
classic tackle on France's
speedy winger Christophe
Domenici.

OPPOSITE Who said all he
could do was kick? Wilkinson
infiltrates the Welsh defences
and leaves Mark Taylor and
Dafydd Jones both clutching
at thin air.

out of puff after giving the favourites one big fright. Wilkinson had a relatively modest 15 points, and it was apparently soon forgotten that England scored four tries to one in that match against a side famous for its running rugby. Critics were looking for flaws to back up a widely-held belief that England would again find a way to lose this Cup, too.

Wilkinson, in a frank interview earlier this year in England, expressed the fears he has harboured of losing since he was old enough to feel anything – that is, when he started playing rugby at four. He confessed that the very thought of losing a tight match used to make him so depressed and nervous he would become physically ill. The nausea would last until kickoff time.

That fear, he believes, has been turned into a tremendous will to win. He is pragmatic about it, talking about simply doing what he is paid to do. He is an undemonstrative man, and certainly not vain. Nobody who was vain could have accepted that IRB award with his shirt collar all over the place and his tie-knot under his ear. His acceptance speech was a model of modesty that never seemed false.

Asked by a television reporter what the 24 hours since victory had been like for Jonny Wilkinson, he replied: "I started off pretty nervous. I'm nervous again now, which I'd rather not be." His girlfriend, actress Diana Stewart, watched proudly from their table. It is typical of Wilkinson that he flatly refuses to discuss anything about their relationship or his private life.

He was reminded of the day in Brisbane when he first confronted Australia to lose 76-0. The journey, it was suggested, had now been completed. He was having none of that.

"I think part of the journey was completed last night. There's more games to come, several more hopefully, and more games to prepare for, try to move forward each time I go out there," he said.

He gave himself a week off, and anyone who knows him knows he will be fretting until he can get back out there on the practice pitch with an armful of rugby balls, resuming the quest for perfection.

Turning points

A burst of individual brilliance, the bounce of an unpredictable ball. A drop goal missed, another safely over. A captain's inspiration, a teammate's consolation. A game, a tournament, the destiny of a Rugby World Cup can turn in the blink of an eye. Here, captured by the camera's eye, are four such moments from RWC 2003.

FIJI v USA, Brisbane, October 15

IF ONLY...

United States fly-half Brian Hercus misses a difficult conversion kick and Fiji wins by a point.

Fiji has lost its opening game to France. Now, with the second match against the United States in injury time, Kort Schubert's try for the USA has made it 19-18 to Fiji. Free-scoring American five-eighth Brian Hercus lines up the conversion kick (below). The angle, out on the touchline, is a difficult one. A distraught Hercus misses and his team is beaten for the second time at RWC 2003, but his teammates have energy left to console him (right). "It is a 15-man game," says USA coach Tom Billups in defence of his star. "It is not Mike's job to win a game at the death." Try telling Hercus that ...

**AUSTRALIA v IRELAND,
November 1,
Melbourne**

**"WE SURVIVED..."
Wallaby skipper George
Gregan gathers his team
and reminds them what
they have done.**
With four minutes of the
final Pool A match
remaining, Ireland's David
Humphreys just misses
a drop goal attempt that
would have put his side
19-17 in front. It is a
gallant Irish side's last
throw of the dice.
Kick-started by Gregan's
own opening drop goal,
Australia have led
throughout, but failed to
put out the Irish fire. Brian
O'Driscoll's try and drop
goal have made the margin
a single point. Australia will
play Scotland in one
quarter-final; Ireland must
now face the rampant
French. As Gregan tells his
unbeaten troops, "We
weren't at our best – but
we survived ..."

FIJI v SCOTLAND, November 1, Sydney

TOO CLOSE FOR COMFORT
Tom Smith's late try saves Scotland as frustrated Fiji bows out.

Rupeni Caucaunibuca's (right) two scintillating tries have exposed the frailties of the Scottish defence. Only Chris Paterson's boot has kept the Scots in it against free-running Fiji and the flying winger, who lead 14-6 at half-time. Three Paterson penalties have Scotland ahead at the 65-minute mark. Two by Nicky Little swing the game Fiji's way again. But with just three minutes remaining, Scotland wins lineout ball close to the Fijian line. Veteran prop Tom Smith plunges over for the equalising try. Paterson, Scotland's top scorer of RWC 2003, does the rest. The men in dark blue celebrate their passage to the quarter-finals (below). The Fijians are homeward bound.

ENGLAND v WALES, November 9, Brisbane

ROBINSON SLAYS THE RED DRAGONS
Brilliant run sets up the try that turns the tide.

The fourth quarter-final is not going according to the script. Wales, with two tries already on the board, are leading by 10 points to three at half-time. This evening, though, St George will come in the diminutive form of flying England fullback Jason Robinson (above). The second half is only four minutes old when his devastating burst of speed cuts through the heart of the Welsh defence. The timing of the pass is exquisite and Will Greenwood (right) gratefully grounds the ball for the solitary English try. Jonny Wilkinson converts, and his boot helps England skip clear. The Red Dragons have been slain, but not without a mighty fight.

A

POOL RESULTS

AUSTRALIA **24** d ARGENTINA **8**
Telstra Stadium, Sydney

IRELAND **45** d ROMANIA **17**
Central Coast Stadium, Gosford

ARGENTINA **67** d NAMIBIA **14**
Central Coast Stadium, Gosford

AUSTRALIA **90** d ROMANIA **8**
Suncorp Stadium, Brisbane

IRELAND **64** d NAMIBIA **7**
Aussie Stadium, Sydney

ARGENTINA **50** d ROMANIA **3**
Aussie Stadium, Sydney

AUSTRALIA **142** d NAMIBIA **0**
Adelaide Oval, Adelaide

IRELAND **16** d ARGENTINA **15**
Adelaide Oval, Adelaide

ROMANIA **37** d NAMIBIA **7**
York Park, Launceston

AUSTRALIA **17** d IRELAND **16**
Telstra Dome, Melbourne

More green than gold

Sweet revenge for Ireland one week, despair the next, and the Pool of Death had been decided.

Three nations ranked in the world's top seven produced an enthralling climax to the group preliminaries, with Ireland the centrepiece on dramatic back-to-back Saturdays against Argentina and Australia.

One-point results in both matches carved Argentina an early passage home, the Wallabies a perceived dream run to the semi-finals, and Ireland a chunky slice from the pie of rugby's mixed emotions.

But there were dress rehearsals to be staged before the decisive jostling took place.

The Wallabies opened the tournament, as host nation and defending champions, against an Argentine side whose forward muscle was expected to stretch the Australians in front of 80,000 at Telstra Stadium.

Lineout woes undermined the Pumas' challenge and the Wallabies, resembling rough diamonds, blundered their way to victory 24-8.

A torrent of errors and butchered opportunities marred the Australian performance while also offering the teasing prospect that there was a gem to be polished if the mistake rate could be reduced.

Number eight David Lyons, handed the role with Toutai Kefu out of the tournament injured, was a first-game revelation, carrying the ball on five occasions inside the first 16 minutes.

But the Australians failed to capitalise on his go-forward efforts. They finished with two tries to one and led only 17-8 with nine minutes remaining.

Argentine five-eighth Felipe Contepomi was successful with just one kick from five. The previous November in Argentina he managed only two from nine against the same opposition.

It provided the Wallabies breathing space the Pumas could ill afford to provide. Hooker Mario Ledesma provided another pressure release with his wayward lineout throwing.

A concern for the Australians was the awkward landing by second-rower David Giffin after taking the second-half kickoff. He damaged a shoulder and would miss the next two matches against Romania and Namibia.

ABOVE One that got away: the Gilbert goes missing from Girvan Dempsey's grasp.

OPPOSITE Unlocked: Australia's David Giffin suffered early injury in the opener against Argentina.

PREVIOUS PAGE Getting the angles right: Australia's Mat Rogers in full cry against Romania.

Ireland opened their campaign the following night in Gosford, ploughing through difficult conditions to dispose of Romania 45-17.

The Romanians offered solid resistance in the forwards, even stealing a tight head. And while they were down 26-0 at half-time, a second-half revival left them in range at the hour mark.

The Irish took more than 20 minutes to register their first try with centre Kevin Maggs, causing havoc in midfield, laying on a try for winger Shane Horgan.

Hooker Keith Wood grabbed another when he took a pass from halfback Peter Stringer and galloped 30 metres.

Fullback Girvan Dempsey, one of Ireland's best, had a hand in two second-half scores as Ireland increased the tempo over the final quarter.

Argentina finished with 10 tries when they handed Namibia their first thrashing three days later at the same NSW Central Coast venue.

Centre Martin Gaitan underlined his speed and finishing qualities with three tries, but it was the Pumas' might up front that fractured the Africans.

There were two pushover tries and two penalty tries from scrums near the Namibian line. The domination extended to the lineout as the Pumas' tight five took control.

Argentina led 27-7 at half-time but, in a beaten side, Namibian halfback Hakkies Husselman displayed the class that has had him playing at the highest levels of South African provincial rugby.

The high scoring continued as the Wallabies took apart Romania 90-8 in Brisbane. Skipper George Gregan predicted the Australians would attack like hungry dogs. And they did remove the muzzles to gorge on 13 tries. There were more handling errors to cause concern, 14 in all. But the second-half dominance, after leading 38-8 at the break, again offered the promise of better to come. The Wallabies equalled their highest-ever winning margin in a Test, alongside the 92-10 win against Spain in Madrid two years earlier.

Thirteen tries equalled an existing record, and Australian centre Elton Flatley knocked over a landmark 11 conversions. He also scored the opening try after just 18 seconds – a Rugby World Cup record.

Ireland also went record-collecting as they beat Namibia 67-7 in the rain at Sydney's Aussie Stadium, where a crowd of more than 35,000 clad themselves in plastic protection to watch the mismatch unfold.

The Irish dominated possession, winger Denis Hickie impressed with his power running wide, and Namibian second-rower Heino Senekal did not help the minnows' cause when he was sin-binned on 20 minutes.

Argentina continued to bruise their way past lesser opposition by re-igniting their scrum fire as Romania was cast aside 50-3.

Another two pushover tries were the reward for the Pumas pack while centre Gaitan, for the second game running, impressed with his midfield pace.

Argentina was 24-0 ahead at the break and scored 21 seconds after the resumption when a clearing kick by Romanian five-eighth Ionut Tofan was charged down.

The Wallabies arrived to play Namibia on Adelaide Oval, the home of cricket in South Australia and the former backyard of the late, great Sir Donald Bradman.

ABOVE Rain dance: Ireland's Denis Hickie hung on to a wet ball as he crossed the line against Namibia.

OPPOSITE Captain Courageous: Romeo Gontineac leads Romania from the front.

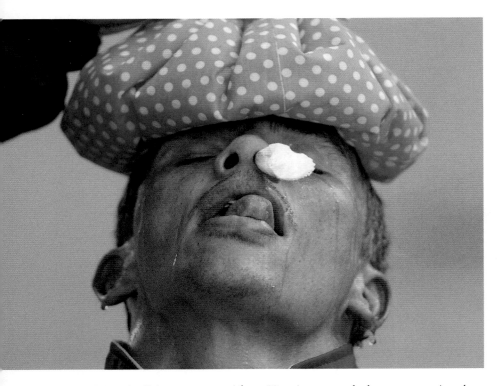

ABOVE Pain and suffering: Ronaldo Pedro did his best to stem the tide that flowed against Namibia.

OPPOSITE Centre stage: Argentina had lots to celebrate with two wins and the narrowest of defeats by Ireland in their final match.

After 53 minutes and three try-scoring hat-tricks the Wallabies had an historic hundred, the first in their 104 years of international competition. The records continued to pile on until the final whistle.

The Wallabies ran in 22 tries, fullback Chris Latham set an Australian record of five tries in a Test, winger Mat Rogers gathered 42 points and, most significantly, Matt Giteau emerged as a five-eighth of future greatness.

Australia swept in for five tries in the opening 15 minutes to lead 33-0.

But what a difference a day makes. The following afternoon, Ireland met Argentina in a match the Pumas had to win to stay in quarter-final contention.

Four years earlier, Argentina had prevented the Irish reaching the last eight by toppling them in a quarter-final qualifier. The pressure was immense. It showed in the arm-wrestle approach that ensued.

Eventually it came down to one point, the Irish winning 16-15 to snare a quarter-final berth and consign the Pumas to an early flight home.

"We played poorly for periods of the game," said skipper Keith Wood. "We seemed to freeze somewhat out there. But there was the weight of expectation that has been building the last four years. The shackles are now off."

Before Ireland had the chance to support Wood's claims, Namibia and Romania were given their time as drawcard attractions in the first Test played in Tasmania.

Romania won 37-7 in Launceston to depart with a prized victory and a fourth-place pool finish.

The script for the group was following the expected path, given the near-hiccup for Ireland in Adelaide. The Australia-Ireland match in Melbourne was not expected to force a re-write.

Skipper Wood spoke of the confidence Ireland had in themselves to do the job on the Wallabies. A full-strength team was named. And an upset almost triggered.

The Wallabies dodged a Rugby World Cup bullet, winning 17-16 in a pulsating finish that bore an eerie resemblance to the RWC 1991 showdown between the two sides in Dublin.

It was a fast, confident start from the Wallabies. They were up 11-3 on 17 minutes. Flanker George Smith, perched on the left wing, had sailed across for a slick try and centre Elton Flatley banged over two penalties.

Then Ireland awoke, realised they were not fighting out of their division, and held up their hands. The Wallabies spent most of the next hour on the ropes.

If Ireland, just once, had replicated the finishing qualities centre sensation Brian O'Driscoll unveiled in the 49th minute to score his side's only try, if five-eighth David Humphreys had landed a long-range attempt at a drop goal inside the final five minutes, it could all have been so different.

The Irish knew an opportunity had passed. Coach Eddie O'Sullivan believed his side had deserved to win, that they had enjoyed forward supremacy only to be denied by a determined Australian defence.

The joy at beating Argentina had been diluted by the realisation that they could also have claimed the world champions' scalp. But Wood and O'Sullivan were not shattered.

They could not afford to be, Wood responded. There was a quarter-final to be won the next week.

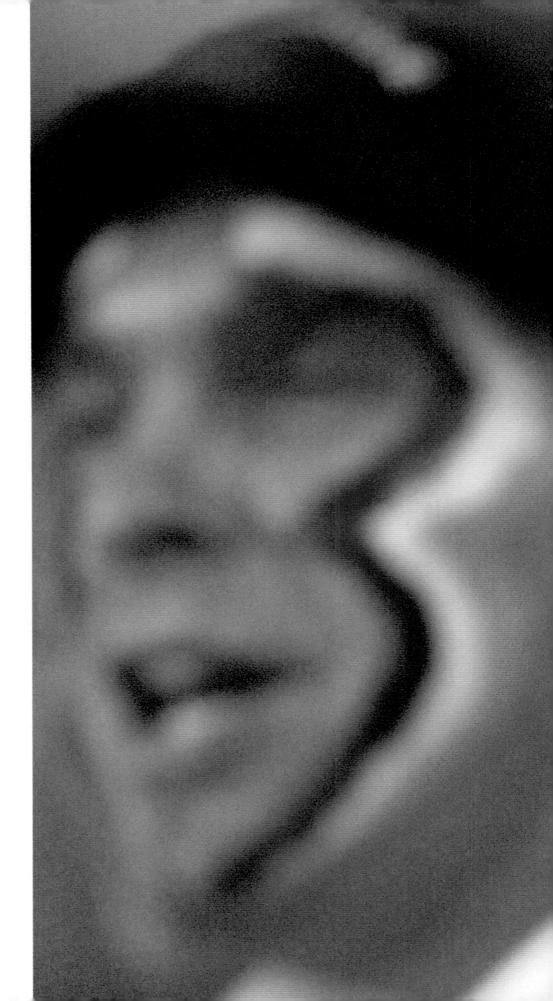

POOL RESULTS

FRANCE **61** d FIJI **18**
Suncorp Stadium, Brisbane

SCOTLAND **32** d JAPAN **11**
Dairy Farmers Stadium, Townsville

FIJI **19** d USA **18**
Suncorp Stadium, Brisbane

FRANCE **51** d JAPAN **29**
Dairy Farmers Stadium, Townsville

SCOTLAND **39** d USA **15**
Suncorp Stadium, Brisbane

FIJI **41** d JAPAN **13**
Dairy Farmers Stadium, Townsville

FRANCE **51** d SCOTLAND **9**
Telstra Stadium, Sydney

JAPAN **26** d USA **39**
Central Coast Stadium, Gosford

FRANCE **41** d USA **14**
WIN Stadium, Wollongong

SCOTLAND **22** d FIJI **20**
Aussie Stadium, Sydney

Michalak attack

The class of the French, the flair of the Fijians, the old-fashioned perseverance of the Scots, the big-hearted performances from the Americans and the unfailing optimism of the Japanese all combined in a fascinating mix which made this one of the most keenly-contested pools, with some of the most thrilling and spectacular games of Rugby World Cup 2003.

And while many will remember the consummate performances of a thoroughly professional French side, perhaps the enduring memories of Pool B will be the extraordinary public support generated for the Japanese team by the people of Townsville. It will also be remembered for the battle for the second quarter-final spot going right down to the wire, with Scotland overcoming the Fijians with less than five minutes to play in the final game of the pool.

France, of course, was the most successful, qualifying top of the pool with a maximum possible 20 points, a performance which was indicative of their domination in the early rounds. From their very first game against Fiji in Brisbane, the French looked a class act, comprehensively beating Fiji 61-18, and producing what was instantly recognised as the best performance ever by a French side in a Rugby World Cup pool match. This was no longer the edgy, temperamental French side of past Rugby World Cups, but a finely-tuned machine capable of absorbing pressure, snuffing out the resistance from their opponents, and scoring some glorious tries while it was at it.

Fly-half Frédéric Michalak, who scored 26 points with the boot in his first Rugby World Cup outing, also sent out a signal that he was a star in the making, not only because he solved the headache of who would be France's goalkicker, but also because of the confident way he directed the play, setting up his outsides perfectly and repeatedly breaking the line with his own individual brilliance.

This game was also memorable for another reason, namely the man with the unforgettable name, Rupeni Caucaunibuca. Billed as one of the potential sensations of the Rugby World Cup 'Caucau', as he is commonly known, gave an early glimpse of his unparalleled attacking gifts, scoring an extraordinary 70-metre try and leaving several French defenders for dead.

Caucau, however, went on to blot his copybook after being cited for punching an opponent and was subsequently banned for two weeks.

Like Caucau, at times the Fijians were sensational, and at others disappointing. Against the Americans, when they were lucky to scrape through with a 19-18 win, they looked lackadaisical,

BELOW France's treatment of the Scots was, like this try, a little Brusque ...

OPPOSITE No, it's not the score: it's a Japanese fan's way of showing what an impression this World Cup made.

PREVIOUS PAGE Wear your colours with pride – this French fan certainly did.

while against Japan they alternated between periods of clumsy play and moments of true genius, as reflected by their centre Seru Rabeni, winger Aisea Tuilevu and their fullback Norman Ligairi, who scored arguably one of the best tries of the competition.

Making something out of nothing 60 metres from the goal-line, Ligairi chipped ahead along the right touch-line. As Japanese defenders scrambled to get the ball, Ligairi toed ahead beautifully and, as the ball stopped only a metre or so from the line, in one smooth, unbroken action, he swooped on it at full speed, scooped it up and dived over in the corner. It was a magical moment, and the triumph of sheer individual brilliance which only the Fijians can produce.

The Japanese deserve special mention, if not for their results, then at least for their indomitable spirit which earned the admiration of rugby-lovers from around the world. Statistics show that they failed to win a game, but they won countless hearts for the way they battled against their more illustrious opponents. With fifteen minutes to play against Scotland for instance, the Japanese were only four points adrift at 15-11; against Fiji they were only three points behind (16-13) at half-time, while against France at one stage in the second half they were only one point behind (20-19), before eventually succumbing to the superior strength, skill and professionalism of the European superpower.

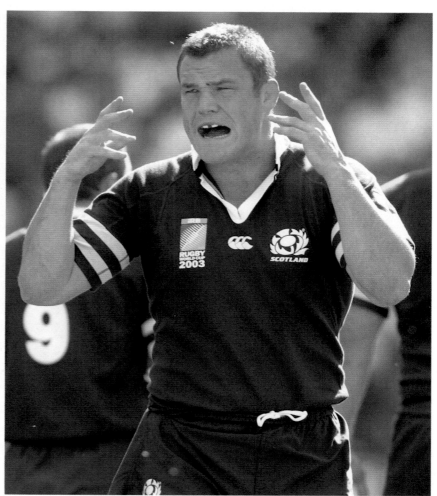

The Americans also did much for the reputation of their rugby, producing four gutsy performances, one of which, their 13-point victory over Japan, broke the longest losing drought at Rugby World Cup: 10 straight losses since 1987. Earlier, they had been desperately unlucky to lose 19-18 against Fiji, and if Mike Hercus' sideline conversion, after a superb injury-time try to Kort Schubert, had gone over, no one would have begrudged them their victory.

In their penultimate game against Japan, however, in what was one of the most spectacular meetings of the opening rounds, the Eagles finally got the rewards they deserved. In front of nearly 20,000 people at Gosford's Central Coast Stadium, both teams threw caution to the winds, and in an absorbing tussle, there was only one point between them with six minutes to play. A try to South African-born winger Riaan van Zyl ended Japan's challenge, however, while hooker Kirk Khasigian added the USA's fifth try to take the final score to 39-26.

While these so-called minnows were desperately saving their honour, the top-of-the-table battle continued between France, Scotland and Fiji. The French put the result beyond doubt when, despite a scrappy game against Japan, they once again raised the bar against Scotland, with a record-breaking 51-9 victory.

This was an even better performance than against Fiji, and suddenly marked France as one of the potential favourites to take the world title. They scored five tries to none, and dominated the Scots in all sectors, proving that they had perhaps the finest forward pack in world rugby, with an immensely powerful tight five, and an equally gifted back three in Serge Betsen, Imanol Harinordoquy (both of whom scored tries from set phases) and Olivier Magne.

ABOVE Gallant in defeat, Japan left the Rugby World Cup stage with many new-found friends.

OPPOSITE It's mine and you can't have it! The USA tried hard to wrest the initiative from some of world rugby's more fancied sides, losing by just one point to Fiji in their opening match.

Indeed, Scotland were the biggest disappointment in this pool. They failed to find the form that had made them look so threatening in South Africa in June 2003, and despite all the experience at their disposal, they looked decidedly ordinary against Japan and USA. So it was that, with France having finished first, the second quarter-final spot hung on the result of the final pool game between Fiji and Scotland in Sydney.

In a sun-drenched Aussie Stadium, the Scots felt the full power of Fijian rugby in a blistering first-half performance from the Pacific islanders. Having served his two-week suspension, Rupeni Caucaunibuca was back on the left wing for Fiji, and with his first touch of the ball he brought the capacity crowd to their feet. Receiving the ball from a long pass, some 30 metres out, despite having little room to move, Caucau's electrifying acceleration saw him simply burst through two tackles to score Fiji's first try.

Shortly before half-time, he struck again with another trade-mark 70-metre dash, bamboozling the first defender – who simply fell over – then trusting his strength and raw speed to break through the lunging tackle of Scottish fullback Glenn Metcalfe to streak to a second try. Fiji were on fire: they led 14-6 at half-time, and could easily have scored at least two more tries.

In the second half, however, Scotland kept hammering away. Fiji gave away simple penalties,

enabling the Scots to claw their way back and take over the lead at 15-14. But Fijian five-eighth Nicky Little also goaled twice from penalties, to give Fiji the lead once again, 20-15. The turning-point no doubt came when English referee Tony Spreadbury awarded a yellow card against Fijian lock Api Naevo in the 76th minute.

From the ensuing line-out close to the Fijian line, the Scots showed all their experience and poise by mauling, and with barely three minutes left on the clock veteran prop Tom Smith plunged over for the try. Chris Paterson converted to take the score to 22-20 and save the day for Scottish rugby. It was a hard call for Fiji, who had done enough to deserve a quarter-final place, but in the end it was the superior discipline of the Scots, the belief in their game plan, and sheer perseverance which won the day.

This result was nevertheless a depressing one for all those who cherish the underdog and value the contribution of countries like Fiji to Rugby World Cup. For, with Fiji pipped at the post, with Samoa having already been eliminated, and with Argentina also absent from the quarter-finals after an even narrower defeat against Ireland, this was the first time in the history of Rugby World Cup that none of the 'minor' nations had made it through to the quarter-finals.

POOL RESULTS

SOUTH AFRICA 72 d **URUGUAY 6**
Subiaco Oval, Perth

ENGLAND 84 d **GEORGIA 6**
Subiaco Oval, Perth

SAMOA 60 d **URUGUAY 13**
Subiaco Oval, Perth

ENGLAND 25 d **SOUTH AFRICA 6**
Subiaco Oval, Perth

SAMOA 46 d **GEORGIA 9**
Subiaco Oval, Perth

SOUTH AFRICA 46 d **GEORGIA 19**
Aussie Stadium, Sydney

ENGLAND 35 d **SAMOA 22**
Telstra Dome, Melbourne

URUGUAY 24 d **GEORGIA 12**
Aussie Stadium, Sydney

SOUTH AFRICA 60 d **SAMOA 10**
Suncorp Stadium, Brisbane

ENGLAND 111 d **URUGUAY 13**
Suncorp Stadium, Brisbane

England expects

There was only one game in this group that mattered. Or so it seemed. And then along came the Samoans, bringing with them a sense of fun, a sense of exuberance and a sense of the unexpected. They proved that it was possible to play rugby with a smile on the face even if there was thunder in every tackle. They proved that it never pays to take things for granted in this modern, high-tech world of rugby where players are conditioned and routines are carefully programmed. If the rugby world ever allows Samoa to disappear off the map then it should hang its head in shame.

Just when this Rugby World Cup was in danger of producing what looked like a series of rather lop-sided matches, Samoa rewrote the script. We all thought that England's match against South Africa at the Subiaco Oval in Perth would be the game of the group. It wasn't a bad effort, to be fair. In fact it was a raw-boned, old-fashioned test match: hard and uncompromising, a probing

examination of character as much as of skill. England prevailed, 25-6, but only after a titanic tussle.

As the Pool C road-show loaded its wagons and headed out of Western Australia we all thought that the carnival might be over. Samoa had not shown that much in their two pool games, a one-sided 60-13 victory over a disappointing Uruguay, followed by another routine romp against Georgia which ended in a 46-9 victory. There had been sporadic flashes of things to come, but the threat was no more than sketchy promise. Flanker Maurie Fa'asavalu had shown scintillating form against Uruguay but faded quickly against Georgia. Those canny half-backs, Rodney So'oialo and Earl Va'a, had looked smooth and classy against Georgia but that was down to the tired, lax Georgian fringe defence, wasn't it?

No, it wasn't. The game against England at Melbourne's Telstra Dome blew away so many preconceptions. It was a glorious affirmation of global rugby. It was a wondrous portrayal of essential rugby virtues too, proof that rugby is a game of heart and soul as much as it is these days about privilege and elitism.

Samoa may not have had millions pumped into their Rugby World Cup preparation. No matter. What Samoa had, money cannot necessarily buy. They believed in themselves and they believed in each other. This was communal rugby, the laying bare of the collective soul. And what a splendid sight it was.

There was a tense narrative, complex character development and an outcome in doubt until the closing stages. England, who trailed 16-13 at the interval, only really wrapped the game up with Phil Vickery's try six minutes from time.

The upshot was that England's lofty ambition to lift the Webb Ellis Cup diminished in the eyes of

BELOW No standing on ceremony: Samoa gave England the fright of their lives before going down 35-22.

OPPOSITE Eye of a needle: Wilkinson's boot brought England 51 of their 144 points in their first three pool matches.

PREVIOUS PAGE Prayers almost answered: Samoa came close to glory in Pool C.

several witnesses, notably the watching Australian and New Zealand camps, both of whom were in town. Mind you, captain Martin Johnson was none too impressed either.

"That was not good enough," said Johnson. "Full credit to Samoa. They could have beaten us. We're not going to win anything if we play like that."

Jonny Wilkinson proved a barometer of English fortunes. He rarely hit any meaningful rhythm, although he was scrabbling for decent possession for long stretches of the first half.

But if that was worrying enough for the many thousands of England fans in the crowd of 50,647, then the sight of Wilkinson having an attack of the wobbles right in front of the posts really set them on edge. Wilkinson missed one kick from point-blank range and only marginally off-centre, the ball striking the left upright. The resulting thud found a hollow echo in the pit of many England stomachs. In all, four kicks failed to find their target.

Samoa captain and No.8 Semo Sititi scored one of the tries of this or any other Rugby World Cup. His touchdown in the sixth minute came at the end

of an 11-phase sequence, the ball passing through 40 pairs of Samoan hands.

England hauled themselves back into the game in time-honored fashion. Neil Back got the touchdown at the end of a driving maul, then referee Jonathan Kaplan awarded a penalty try against Samoa in the 52nd minute.

"That was a turning-point," said Sititi.

England closed out the game with two tries in the last 11 minutes from Iain Balshaw and Phil Vickery and were relieved to have come through with a 35-22 victory.

"Samoa asked us questions that we have not been asked for a long, long time," said captain Martin Johnson. "We had to dig ourselves out of a hole. We were 10-0 down and hadn't touched the ball. We made too many mistakes and need to look at ourselves as players."

His words found an echo in those of head coach Clive Woodward. "The only people who gave Samoa due credit beforehand were ourselves with our strong selection," said Woodward.

Perhaps the most significant words of the night, and of the entire pool stages, came from

ABOVE Heroic effort: England's relieved players congratulate Samoa captain Semo Sititi and his men after their epic encounter in Melbourne.

OPPOSITE Jaque Fourie claimed three of the 27 tries South Africa ran in during its pool matches.

the Samoa coach, the deeply impressive John Boe.

"We'd like to think that we made a statement tonight and that statement is that our team deserves to survive," said Boe.

There was not a murmur of dissent.

Samoa could not repeat the trick the following week against South Africa. They made more mistakes in the first ten minutes than they had in the entire tournament. South Africa took full advantage, leading 31-3 at the break. There was a stirring Samoan revival in the third quarter but they were hanging on at the final whistle as they went down to a 60-10 defeat.

The Springboks gave their all in an effort to upset England. There was none of the naked aggression that had been on show at Twickenham 11 months earlier. South Africa conducted themselves with splendid forthrightness throughout the build-up week, ducking no issues. Corne Krige did much to redeem himself, as captain and as player, nowhere more conspicuously than when he and his team came up against Martin Johnson's England.

South Africa and England stood toe-to-toe for an hour. England were in trouble in the scrum and could make little headway across the gain line. But they had Jonny Wilkinson. Even though he too was faltering by his own high standards in open field play, his radar was spot-on when it came to sticking the ball between the posts. He didn't miss a kick all evening, finishing with 20 points. In contrast, Louis Koen saw four attempts slide by the posts in the first half.

The moment that England scored their opportunist try in the 62nd minute, their game lifted while South Africa's wilted. Will Greenwood's snaffling follow-up toe-poke and touchdown of

LEFT Cornerstones of the Uruguayan XV, Aguirre and Menchaca were their joint top scorers at 13 points apiece.

FAR LEFT Georgia managed just one try, but no wonder they are happy: it came against the might of South Africa.

Lewis Moody's block on a Louis Koen clearance broke the South African resistance. Wilkinson plunged in the stiletto with two smartly-taken drop goals shortly afterwards.

It was an emphatic scoreline.

The two other teams in Pool C emerged with credit. Samoa had too much class and pace for both, beating Uruguay 60-13 and Georgia 46-9.

Georgia, a tough forward outfit intelligently led by No.8 Ilia Zedguinidze, made sure that England had plenty of bruises the morning after their 84-6 victory. The scoreboard didn't tell the full story of that testing encounter.

The Georgians were unable to sustain their full-bore game throughout the pool stages despite putting up a magnificent show against South Africa before going down 46-19. However, they were almost a spent force by the time they came up against Uruguay four days later, the South Americans winning 24-12 and scoring three tries in the process. Georgia would have hoped for more but the experience of the Uruguayans in their second appearance at a Rugby World Cup saw them home.

Uruguay, well led by centre Diego Aguirre and with No.8 Rodrigo Capo an influential presence, had targeted that game. They had subsided tamely to Samoa, 60-13, and were desperate not to draw a blank.

"That was our final," said Aguirre.

Just as well. England, refreshed and hungry, awaited them in their final pool game. Uruguay, not surprisingly, were put through the mincer, England posting its Rugby World Cup record score in winning 111-13.

POOL RESULTS

NEW ZEALAND **70** d ITALY **7**
Telstra Dome, Melbourne

WALES **41** d CANADA **10**
Telstra Dome, Melbourne

ITALY **36** d TONGA **12**
Canberra Stadium, Canberra

NEW ZEALAND **68** d CANADA **6**
Telstra Dome, Melbourne

WALES **27** d TONGA **20**
Canberra Stadium, Canberra

ITALY **19** d CANADA **14**
Canberra Stadium, Canberra

NEW ZEALAND **91** d TONGA **7**
Suncorp Stadium, Brisbane

WALES **27** d ITALY **15**
Canberra Stadium, Canberra

CANADA **24** d TONGA **7**
WIN Stadium, Wollongong

NEW ZEALAND **53** d WALES **37**
Telstra Stadium, Sydney

Kiwi carnival

New Zealand were, as expected, the big winners and Wales the big movers when the Rugby World Cup's Pool D was played out.

The All Blacks scored more tries (42) and more points (282) than any team in any pool in the tournament, showing a consistency of performance against all their rivals. Both these figures were Rugby World Cup records for pool play.

But the main focus in this group was always going to be on who would finish second behind one of the tournament favourites and claim the other quarter-final berth.

Wales, Italy, Tonga and Canada all talked up their chances before coming to Australia, and reiterated their claims on arrival. With world rankings separating the four teams by just six places, there was every reason for Pool D to have a real air of expectation about it.

Tonga and Canada dropped off the pace early, leaving Six Nations rivals Wales and Italy to battle it out for the playoffs berth behind the All Blacks.

That match – Italy's last and Wales' penultimate pool game – wasn't pretty. But with the stakes so high, it was foolish to expect anything else.

Wales snuck home 27-15 in a dogged affair in Canberra, reversing the result from earlier in the year that left them bottom of the Six Nations table.

A week later, they fronted up to the All Blacks in Sydney and produced one of the best pool matches in the tournament. Their quarter-finals place already secure, Welsh coach Steve Hansen rested most of his frontline players, but his second-stringers played with a power and precision that brought back memories of some of the great Welsh sides of the '70s. They led New Zealand within

BELOW What hit me? Gareth Thomas of Wales discovers the Kiwis can defend as well.

OPPOSITE One more, please: flying winger Doug Howlett scored six tries in the All Blacks' dominant Pool D performance.

PREVIOUS PAGE Catch me if you can: Italy's Sergio Parisse was one of the stars of the pool stage.

CANADA 6 · · ITALY 6

ABOVE In Canberra the Canadians produced a capital performance, making Italy fight all the way for their 19-14 win.

OPPOSITE Dafydd – one of five Jones boys in the Welsh squad – welcomes another score for the Red Dragons.

sight of the final whistle before being over-run 53-37 in the dying stages.

Considering how low Wales has slipped over the past decade or so, this was a fantastic performance. Importantly, making the last eight of the tournament was a worthy achievement for a squad that Hansen has managed to maximize in terms of talent and commitment.

Wales went to Australia with all sorts of doubters back in the valleys, yet came away from pool play with its reputation enhanced.

"It's hard to describe the sort of pressure we have been under," said Hansen. "Qualifying for the quarter-finals was our first goal and represents a good achievement."

Proud of his team's performance against New Zealand, his homeland, Hansen said the All Blacks' ability to absorb the pressure and respond in the final minutes demonstrated the gap that still existed between Wales and the top tier of rugby nations.

And the All Blacks, bar the hiccup of about 45 minutes midway through their match with Wales, certainly did sizzle. Their outside backs came to Australia with big reputations and demonstrated why in pool play. Fullback Mils Muliaina (six tries) and wings Doug Howlett (six) and Joe Rokocoko (four) were all try-scoring machines with their speed, steps and swerves the key to finishing off when given an inch of space.

The All Blacks lost their vice-captain Tana Umaga with a knee injury after just 26 minutes of their opening game against Italy and spent the next three matches trying to sort out a new-look midfield that would keep capitalising on that outside talent once the playoffs arrived.

It was a tricky process, but utility Leon MacDonald eventually displaced back-up centre Ma'a Nonu, aided by a deadly goalkicking boot that saw him land his first 16 attempts in succession.

So the black machine marched on, although the splutters against Wales would have given all their major opponents for the title some heart, as there was some vulnerability to a team that had looked so impressive in claiming the Tri-Nations title earlier in the year with an unblemished record against South Africa and Australia.

The Italians headed home with mixed emotions. Two wins from pool play represented their best Rugby World Cup effort in five tournaments. But coach John Kirwan – another Kiwi – knew the Azzurri had blown a real chance to reach the quarter-finals for the first time with their loss to Wales.

He had orchestrated a clever campaign, sacrificing the opening game against New Zealand to give his side the chance to kick-start their run with a vital 36-12 win over Tonga. The 19-14 effort over Canada set up their playoffs tilt before they fell at the final hurdle against Wales.

But Kirwan managed to unearth a bright new star, albeit a 27-year-old from the second division of Italian club rugby. Rima Wakarua was Kirwan's selection bolter, and he played the vital fly-half role with all the assurance of a Test veteran. He had a good left boot that netted 50 points and also drove the Italian forwards in the right direction with his field kicking.

"I think the Rugby World Cup has been a real positive for Italian rugby. It's our job now to keep getting better," said Kirwan.

"We need to turn this positive Rugby World Cup into a positive Six Nations."

Kirwan's thoughts echoed many from a pool where hopes were always going to be higher than reality.

At the bottom, Canada outplayed Tonga 24-7 in the final match to send the wooden spoon home to the Pacific islands. A Rugby World Cup victory was a fitting finale for Canada's retiring veteran captain Al Charron, not that he would remember much of it after being knocked unconscious early in the game.

There's no doubt that Canada have the structure in their game to beat teams of similar ability. They showed once again they have power up front and good direction in the halves. Yet a lack of resources has seen them unable to reach the lofty heights of their quarter-final appearance in 1991 in the ensuing years.

Their Australian coach Dave Clark, who also bowed out at the tournament, made a plea for greater support and said that involved the need for

more quality international matches for the Canadians. He believed the Pacific Rim tournament must be resurrected to help rugby in the Americas, Asia and the South Pacific.

They were, he said, the areas with the greatest growth potential if rugby was to enhance the depth of top talent for future Rugby World Cups.

Tongan coach Jim Love grew increasingly frustrated at the inability of his team to play to its potential as the pool stage developed. Love brought far better discipline to the Tongan team than they had displayed at previous Rugby World Cups, but they were shaded in the flair department by their island neighbours Samoa and Fiji, who came so very close to qualifying for the playoffs.

So, for a pool that had many permutations to it before the tournament started, the Rugby World Cup saw normal transmission resume. The All Blacks were comfortably the best, the Welsh resurrection continued, Italy went home half-happy, while Canada and Tonga were left to ponder their options.

ABOVE Tonga tried manfully but discipline and effort were not enough and they left empty-handed, although Heamani Lavaka got plenty of Canada's James Pritchard here.

OPPOSITE With 42 tries, New Zealand crossed the line 12 times more often than the other four Pool D nations put together. Fullback Mils Muliaina grabbed six himself.

QUARTER-FINALS

QUARTER-FINAL RESULTS

QUARTER-FINAL 1
NEW ZEALAND **29** d SOUTH AFRICA **9**
Telstra Dome, Melbourne

QUARTER-FINAL 2
AUSTRALIA **33** d SCOTLAND **16**
Suncorp Stadium, Brisbane

QUARTER-FINAL 3
FRANCE **43** d IRELAND **21**
Telstra Dome, Melbourne

QUARTER-FINAL 4
ENGLAND **28** d WALES **17**
Suncorp Stadium, Brisbane

BY DUNCAN JOHNSTONE (*SPORTSCAST*, AUCKLAND)

Forward march

Revenge has rarely tasted sweeter for the All Blacks than their Rugby World Cup quarter-final win over the Springboks in Melbourne.

There aren't too many records that have eluded the All Blacks down the long path of their proud history, but a Rugby World Cup win over South Africa was one and so was crossing the Boks' try-line at the game's biggest tournament.

To eradicate both those glaring omissions in such emphatic fashion was certainly satisfying for New Zealand and its fans.

The 29-9 scoreline was a three-tries-to-none result. And there was a real feeling that the scoreline could have been even greater but for a couple of handling lapses when tries were beckoning.

But that is nit-picking over an All-Black performance that was a huge leap forward from their pool play, especially against such a distinguished opponent.

This won't have wiped out the pain of the RWC 1995 final loss the Springboks inflicted on the All Blacks, nor the embarrassment of the defeat they handed New Zealand in the playoff for third four years later in Wales.

But the stakes were high in this match, with both teams looking to avoid their earliest Rugby World Cup departures. It was the Springboks who took the plane home, with the All Blacks stepping on a domestic flight to Sydney for the semi-finals. And in their luggage was a growing feeling that John Mitchell's team had a real shot at taking the Webb Ellis Cup back over the Tasman Sea.

Certainly in defeating South Africa they showed a well-rounded armoury. The Springboks

RIGHT Staring down the barrel: South African Faan Rautenbach has that sinking feeling as New Zealand extends its lead.

PREVIOUS PAGE Picture perfect: Frédéric Michalak slots another conversion for France.

were relying on their big pack to dominate and allow young fly-half Derick Hougaard to dictate.

But such was the power and accuracy of the All Blacks' pack, bolstered by the return of their world-class lock Chris Jack, that it was almost 10 minutes before the Boks could even get their hands on the ball. New Zealand's lineout was spot-on, their scrum rock-solid and the loose forward play of Richie McCaw and Jerry Collins simply outstanding.

And they also revealed a new star in hooker Keven Mealamu, whose driving play was relentless and would ultimately be rewarded with a 23-metre try that sealed the match.

"Many people underestimate the ability of our forward pack who sometimes don't get the

rewards they're due. They were superb tonight," said a delighted Mitchell after the win.

With the forwards so dominant, Justin Marshall and Carlos Spencer were able to control the match from the halves. Spencer, like the All Blacks' pack, went up a gear in this match. Spurred by the occasion, he unleashed all his skills and all his cheek. By the end of the match he was practically taunting the Boks with his passing.

It was a Spencer break that led to New Zealand's historic first try, with centre Leon MacDonald running off the fly-half's shoulder for a clear run to the line.

All the other New Zealand first-half points came from MacDonald's boot as the All Blacks led

machine Joe Rokocoko the easiest of his five tournament touchdowns so far.

Victory was New Zealand's and it was one to relish.

"This is right up there," said Mitchell. "There's nothing better as a New Zealander, I believe, than playing the Springboks. For us as coaches to be involved in something like this is special."

The Boks were gracious in defeat. Really, they had no alternative – they were soundly beaten in every facet of the game.

"They played very good rugby. I'm disappointed, but we were beaten by a better team. We couldn't get our hands on the ball. I haven't played a New Zealand team like that before," were the words from Joost van der Westhuizen, the halfback who has played more games against the All Blacks than any other Springbok.

The loss meant the end of van der Westhuizen's international career. He had twice tasted World Cup victory over the All Blacks, including getting his hands on the Webb Ellis Cup in '95.

But now it was the All Blacks who had the chance to get their hands back on the golden prize with this historic win. Everyone knew they had the backs to do the damage, but against the Boks they showed they also had the grunt and determination up front.

LEFT For once the Springboks collar Kiwi Leon MacDonald. But the big centre broke free to score 16 of his side's 29 points.

ABOVE For Joe Rokocoko, try five of the tournament was his most straight-forward to date.

13-6 at the break, South Africa managing only two Hougaard penalties from rare raids into Kiwi territory.

The seven-point difference held till the 59-minute mark as the Boks displayed dogged defence. But Mealamu worked his magic, bursting clear from a maul just outside the South African 22 and using his power and low centre of gravity to charge to the line.

Another MacDonald penalty in the 67th minute gave New Zealand breathing space at 24-9.

Then in the dying stages Spencer displayed his outrageous skills. Skipper Reuben Thorne turned over possession on the Boks' line and Spencer flicked a pass between his legs to give try-scoring

Halfway there

It was two days after the Wallabies advanced, unconvincingly it must be said, to the tournament's final four. Ireland coach Eddie O'Sullivan was reflecting on his own side's departure from the knockout stages when the conversation drifted to the Australians.

According to O'Sullivan, whose side had come within a point of the host nation only a week before, the Wallabies were caving in under the pressure of defending the Rugby World Cup on familiar soil.

"The pressure on the players and the coaching staff is phenomenal and I think that is working against them at the moment," he said. "They are being suffocated at the moment by expectation and that can strangle anybody. They are being watched and assessed on everything they do and it's claustrophobic. It's holding back the team. If they could just shake that pressure off and go out and play rugby they're as good as anyone in the world."

Certainly in beating Scotland by 17 points, after being held to 9-all at the break, the Wallabies were not as good as anyone in the world. They were not as good as the other three teams left standing, a notion bookmakers also embraced by installing the Australians as rank outsiders for the title after the three tries to one result.

But in seeing off the Scots, the Wallabies had their semi-final berth and RWC 2003 organisers their dream showdown. After a nightmare first half, where blunders walked hand-in-hand with the RWC 1999 champions, there were no guarantees the Wallabies were going to squeeze past Scotland and into a penultimate clash with the All Blacks.

Eventually they prevailed. There was some fluency from the Wallabies in the second stanza. It could not, however, camouflage the concerns that mounted during the ghastly opening 40 minutes. To give the Australians their due, they did try to attack with width. But coach Eddie Jones must have cringed as he watched his plans slowly shredded by another bucketload of backline bungles.

Fullback Mat Rogers reached his trademark quota of two fumbles per game inside the opening half-hour. The first he dropped stone cold when heading for open pastures and with an unmarked Wendell Sailor in support. Sailor joined the sweaty hands contest, losing his share of possession, if mostly in the tackle.

There were angles run, decoys employed, and opportunities presented. But the Wallabies failed to

BELOW 'This one's mine': Australian winger Wendell Sailor makes sure Scotland's Simon Danielli has nowhere to go.

OPPOSITE Hemispheres apart: Wallaby skipper George Gregan follows his own kick ahead to score a try, former Scottish counterpart Gordon Bulloch reads the writing on the wall.

ABOVE It's showtime as Stirling Mortlock makes the most of his return to score Australia's opening try of the match.

OPPOSITE 'I know it's your last international, but I'll give the orders': referee Steve Walsh lays down the law to Scotland skipper Bryan Redpath.

finish. They had also forgotten how to sustain momentum. The ideas were there. But, to steal a Jones buzzword, the execution was missing.

But the malaise behind the scrum was not as frightening as what was occurring at the lineout. It was knee-trembling stuff for hooker Brendan Cannon every time he stepped to the touchline. Australia tried short lineouts, they went for full numbers. They did everything they could to turn the tide of Scottish domination.

The pressure from the Scottish forwards at scrum and lineout helped them pin the Wallabies inside their own half for much of the opening stanza. A shoulder injury to flanker George Smith forced a half-time substitution for the more vertically-advantaged Matt Cockbain.

The only points for the Australians in the first stanza came from the boot of inside centre Elton Flatley. But his three penalty goals were cancelled out by two from Scottish five-eighth Chris Paterson, who also landed a monstrous drop goal from 49 metres. A knock to the head during the pre-game warm-up had left Paterson needing to be helped from the field dazed and wobbly, but luckily did not carry any long-lasting effects.

Five minutes into the second half, with the two sides level, Australia finally found some order to their game. Returning outside centre Stirling Mortlock gave the Wallabies their first try with a solo effort from 55 metres out. But to praise the individuality of the scorer is to ignore how the ball came to be in his hands.

Flanker Phil Waugh, whose gophering work at the breakdown was superb, emerged from a tackle and sent the ball to second-rower Justin Harrison. Harrison sent it on to Flatley, whose pass to

Mortlock was high and to his left. He plucked it from the air without losing stride, found the gap between two defenders and raced untouched to score.

Winger Lote Tuqiri had been the most threatening of the Australian backs, so it was fitting he played a role in the second try, to skipper George Gregan, that effectively shut out the Scots at the 58-minute mark. There was a stutter and a step, and a series of swerves until Tuqiri had taken play almost from the touchline to under the posts. When the ball squirted out of the ruck, Gregan cleverly toed

it ahead and touched down. Number eight David Lyons bullocked across from the back of a scrum six minutes later and Australia was cruising at 33-9.

But the Scots produced one late act of resistance in a match that brought down the playing careers of two long-serving stalwarts in halfback Bryan Redpath and winger Kenny Logan. The final score of the match, in the final minute, was a try to replacement hooker Rob Russell and a conversion from Paterson.

At least the Scots left with heads held high.

French lesson

After their heart-stopping performance against Australia in the final pool game, the Irish were expected to test France in the second quarter-final at Melbourne's Telstra Dome. But in this Northern Hemisphere shoot-out, there was only one team on the park, as the mighty French had too much firepower for the Irish.

Playing at breathtaking speed, and spreading the game as wide as possible right from the word go, France simply had too much class, too much pace, and too many game-breakers for Ireland to match them. For all intents and purposes, the game was over by half-time.

Just as the All Blacks had done the day before against the Springboks, the French played with a precision and intensity which the Irish simply could not match.

Admittedly the French had a dream start, with Olivier Magne crossing for a try after only three minutes of play. But it was the ease with which the French scored which was the most surprising, as a move they had been practising at training all week worked to perfection. From a lineout in Irish territory, the French moved the ball wide. Fullback Nicolas Brusque took the tackle and from the ensuing ruck Fabien Galthié fed five-eighth Frédéric Michalak,

BELOW French captain Fabien Galthié, in a rich vein of form at RWC 2003, launches another attack.

OPPOSITE Ireland's outgoing captain Keith Wood rallies his troops as France seizes the early initiative.

86

ABOVE Tears for souvenirs: Ireland's inspirational captain Keith Wood comes to terms with the end of his outstanding career.

OPPOSITE TOP Too little, too late: brilliant centre Brian O'Driscoll scored the last two of Ireland's three tries but the French were out of reach.

OPPOSITE BOTTOM It's not No.1, it's No.3: Imanol Harinordoquy flies through the air to score France's third try with the greatest of ease.

one to Christophe Dominici after a thrilling counter-attack from the French 22, and the other to Harinordoquy – before half-time. France led 27-0 at the break, and went even further ahead with a penalty to Michalak, then a try to prop forward Jean-Jacques Crenca, duly converted by Michalak, and the scoreboard read 37-0 after only 47 minutes of play. "When I looked up and saw the score, I couldn't believe it," said Magne afterwards. "After all, this was a World Cup quarter-final and we were playing Ireland ... I would never have dreamed of such a score."

"We didn't know what had hit us," commented Irish coach Eddie O'Sullivan. "The French scrum was incredibly powerful, they completely out-muscled us up front and we were completely punch-drunk after 30 minutes. They strangled us to death for the best part of 60 minutes. The French have always had flair and power, but this French team is different: they have a clarity of thought which makes them very menacing."

With the result beyond all doubt, the French started to ease up, allowing Ireland to come back into the game in the final quarter. Showing some of the character that had stood them in good stead in their two one-point finishes against Argentina and Australia, the Irish scored an excellent try to centre Kevin Maggs, who sliced through the French defence on the reverse angle before sprinting away to score beneath the posts.

And, after Michalak had calmly added another penalty, the incomparable Brian O'Driscoll picked up Ireland's second try by following up on a clever grubber-kick from replacement five-eighth David Humphreys.

At 40-14, the score began to look a little more respectable for the Irish, who started to take advantage of the drop-off in the French concentration, as well as the yellow card awarded against Raphael Ibanez for killing the ball in the ruck. Michalak goaled again from a penalty, to give him a 100 per cent strike rate and, with 23 points from the game, take his personal tally at RWC 2003 to 101 points.

But Ireland had the last word, with O'Driscoll

who calmly switched directions, kicking a long, lobbing punt diagonally across to the right wing.

Who should be waiting for it, but No.8 Imanol Harinordoquy? He beat Girvan Dempsey to the ball, fed inside to Tony Marsh, who passed outside to Magne and the flanker jogged over to score unopposed. It was slick, creative and highly skilled, and it gave the French the confidence they needed to play their natural game.

Dominating the lineouts and overpowering Ireland in the scrums, the French monopolised possession, running in two more scintillating tries –

again showing his uncanny instinct for try-scoring, this time from a quick penalty five metres out from the French line, and Humphreys converting, to take the score to 43-21.

It was, however, far too little and far too late for Ireland, and the game ended in emotional scenes as Galthié, the French captain, embraced his opposite number, Keith Wood, as he left the field.

"The French pressurised us in every facet of the game, and to an extent that no other team has," admitted Wood afterwards, as he announced his retirement from all rugby. "To be frank, we were only just hanging on. It could have been one of the worst of days, but we showed some great character in the second half. As for the French, they just played and played and played, and took every point that came their way."

Catt-like tread

Never mind the land of their fathers being proud of them. The whole of planet rugby felt a warm after-glow from this wonderful match. Wales brought colour and verve, wild fancy and unbreakable spirit to the occasion. It brought twinkling feet as well, scoring three tries to England's one.

The Grand Slam champions were beaten senseless for long stretches of the first half by the Six Nations' wooden spoonists. The transformation in fortunes was scarcely credible.

The game was eventually won through England's concerted drive and cussedness and, inevitably, the boot of Jonny Wilkinson. As Wales chased, so it infringed. Wilkinson took due retribution with six penalties; he also picked a ball off his toes in the final second to drop a 40-metre goal.

The game turned when England decided to bring on Mike Catt at half-time. The Bath old-stager stayed true to his roots, playing what was in front of him and not what was programmed into his head.

What instructions had he been given at the interval with England on the rack, trailing 10-3?

"Nothing really, " said Catt, a late selection for the original squad after Alex King pulled out with injury.

"I was just told to go out and play my game. It was a question of going back to basics. We had to cut out our mistakes and just get on with it."

Catt gave England much-needed poise and direction, claiming valuable tracts of territory with his kicking from hand.

At times England looked a shambles. Their first-half display saw them bunched time and again

BELOW The faces tell the story: As England's all-powerful forwards line up to applaud Wales off the field, the Red Dragons know this was a great chance gone begging.

OPPOSITE Gracious in defeat, and in the final international of his career, try-scoring Welsh skipper Colin Charvis congratulates relieved England captain Martin Johnson.

in a narrow-side channel, forcing passes under pressure and making little headway.

There was a catalogue of disturbing errors. Dan Luger, a late call-up after the double withdrawals of Josh Lewsey and Iain Balshaw, was jittery and off-key. He dropped balls and hit a horrendous sliced clearance just before the interval. It was no surprise when his place was taken by Catt in the second half.

Ben Cohen will also look back in horror at his cross-kick from a tap penalty under the Welsh posts in the 25th minute. England was guaranteed three points from that position, yet Cohen grabbed the ball and punted left. Small problem: out there was

the smallest England player, Neil Back, up against the strapping Llanelli wing Mark Jones.

"No, I wouldn't have made that decision if I'd been on the pitch, " said England head coach Clive Woodward. "Ben wasn't thinking too cleverly."

Nor were many others. Mike Tindall's angled kick in the 35th minute pitted lock Ben Kay up against wispy Welsh wing, Shane Williams. It was no contest. From just inside his own 22, Williams backed himself. He made serious ground, scrum-half Gareth Cooper took it on and found Gareth Thomas in support. From there, Williams got in on the act again, juggling the ball before flicking infield to Stephen

initial retrieve deep in his 22, but was then judged to have hung on to the ball. Wales kicked for touch rather than for the posts and were rewarded when Colin Charvis was driven over. Two tries in four minutes and England was reeling.

It was 10-3 at the interval. But Catt's arrival changed England's fortunes. They were back on level terms within three minutes following a sensational 60-metre break from Robinson, who had fielded a clearance kick from Cooper.

Wales had shackled Robinson well all evening. Not this time. He sliced through three attempted tackles and zipped outside two other defenders. The final pass was measured and Greenwood dived in at the corner for his 30th try for England.

Then Catt and Wilkinson got to work. Wales became reckless and ill-disciplined. It gave away 17 penalties, a heinous crime when Old Dead-Eye is in opposition. By the 65th minute, Wilkinson had given England clear water on the scoreboard with five successive kicks.

England ought to have closed out the game, but didn't. Hooker Steve Thompson conceded a penalty, allowing Wales to kick downfield. From the lineout it attacked one way then, when the ball was brought back, Ceri Sweeney's kick high and to the left saw Lawrence Dallaglio clamber back alongside Shane Williams. The ball ricocheted backwards where Martyn Williams was able to swoop and touch down.

Wales couldn't quite bring off the jackpot coup. Iestyn Harris scuffed a kickable penalty six minutes from time. Wilkinson was, by now, in his element.

Fortune had favoured England.

ABOVE Hands up if you're happy! Welsh players salute as skipper Charvis forces his way over and the Red Dragons roar into a 10-3 halftime lead.

OPPOSITE Put your shirt on England – that's what these fervent fans have done, and their confidence was repaid with another fighting win.

Jones who touched down. It was a try to rank with any of the vintage Welsh scores from down the years.

Wales played smart rugby. It had worked out England long ago. Coach Steve Hansen knew that he had to put width on the ball and stretch England's defence, which clusters in midfield. It worked a treat. For all the fine effort, though, Wales came off second-best.

"When you get as close as we have," said Hansen, "it's gut-wrenching to lose. But I hope we've put a smile on the face of Welsh rugby."

A downfield hoof from Cooper led to Wales' second try in the 35th minute. Cohen made the

SEMI-FINALS

SEMI-FINAL RESULTS

SEMI-FINAL 1
AUSTRALIA **22** d NEW ZEALAND **10**
Telstra Stadium, Sydney

SEMI-FINAL 2
ENGLAND **24** d FRANCE **7**
Telstra Stadium, Sydney

Gold standard

The Wallabies believed when almost everyone else had lost the faith and delivered a miracle to carry them to history's doorstep – one game from consecutive global championships.

There was no formline to suggest what would unfold at Telstra Stadium on an evening when the home side thrived in Sydney's heat and finally found its misplaced blowtorch to burn the All Blacks 22-10.

Australia had lost four of five internationals leading into the tournament. It had escaped Melbourne with a one-point win over Ireland in its last pool match and was 9-all at halftime against Scotland before breaking free in the second half of a Brisbane quarter-final.

Hardly the stuff to create widespread confidence that when they faced their biggest challenge of the past four years, a match against an All Blacks side stamped as the benchmark of the modern game, they could suddenly find another level.

Coach Eddie Jones disagreed, believing the so-called quantum leap was not as great as suggested. Few who witnessed the transformation were of the same mindset. But, again, it was defence that won the day. In 1999, the Wallabies based their success on being able to shut down rivals. They did the same in this semi-final.

"They defended with their lives," said shattered All-Black skipper Reuben Thorne. "They put on pressure, we lost our composure."

The All Blacks, for all their flair and breathtaking pace, were hardly in the contest, rarely able to escape the Australian shackles. Significantly, the Wallabies' pack dominated possession battles.

PREVIOUS PAGE
Breakaway – but it's not a forward, it's Wallaby centre Stirling Mortlock intercepting a Carlos Spencer pass to dive through for Australia's opening score against New Zealand.

OPPOSITE The gesture tells it all: Lote Tuqiri had a thumb in every pie as a fired-up Australian side confounded its legion of critics and thrilled its army of fans.

The backline swapped potential for performance but the forwards were the game-day heroes.

Jones and captain George Gregan had boldly outlined their "Big Sting" plans the day before the match. They warned a massive performance was imminent, they hinted at camouflaged tactics, and they told how the side had no fear of the All Blacks.

There were sniggers from those whose faith had waned.

But the pre-empted surprises were unwrapped early. Australia ran the ball from inside its own quarter and kept it in hand through more than half a dozen phases, running down the first two minutes on the clock. Then they kept running, attacking key targets.

They had forwards roaming wide, five-eighth Stephen Larkham was taking the ball to the line and centre Stirling Mortlock was all pumping legs and tackle-breaking power.

He would score the Wallabies' only try of the game, in the ninth minute, intercepting a trademark wide pass from Kiwi playmaker Carlos Spencer and racing 85 metres to touch down.

But Mortlock's impact stretched well beyond his five-point contribution. He was the arrowhead as the Wallabies made All Blacks' outside centre Leon MacDonald a major target.

The Kiwi is not a specialist in the position. It was a weakness Jones wanted to exploit and Mortlock did the job.

When the All Blacks tried to rally, they were

smashed into error. Flankers George Smith and Phil Waugh nullified the danger of No.8 Jerry Collins, while All-Black hooker Keven Mealamu, a crucial go-forward exponent, did not carry the ball until the 17th minute.

Another setback to the Kiwis was the rib cartilage damage sustained by halfback Justin Marshall after he was hit from behind in a tackle by Smith. The Australian was penalised for a late shot, but the damage was already done. Marshall struggled on until the 47th minute, when he was replaced by Byron Kelleher.

Around the same time, Australian prop Ben Darwin was lifted off his feet in a scrum and twisted awkwardly. He heard a crack and screamed immediately "Neck, neck, neck". All Blacks' rival Kees Meeuws backed off and Darwin collapsed to the ground.

For two horrifying minutes he lost all feeling below his neck. He would eventually regather sensation in his arms and legs but was rushed to a Sydney hospital spinal ward and remained there for several days. His Rugby World Cup was over.

The biggest game of Darwin's life had gone horribly awry but, considering the worst-case scenario that could have occurred as a disc in his neck burst from its casing and pressed on his spinal cord, he was relieved later to have survived the on-field scare.

In some respects then, the New Zealand woes could be put in the perspective that they only lost a game of rugby. Try telling that, though, to a nation in mourning.

The Kiwi lineout caught the ills the Wallabies had previously experienced. Four crooked throws and two steals were the ugly statistics they had to view as another Rugby World Cup campaign turned to ash.

There was one try for the Kiwis, when a turnover was punished by a searching run from Spencer. He sent flanker Reuben Thorne across the line. It pulled the score back to 13-7 on 34 minutes. But this was a

night when the Wallabies shut out the match.

Inside centre Elton Flatley converted pressure to points, kicking five penalty goals – three of them after halftime – and a conversion.

"They didn't let us play our game," said Spencer.

And those few words encapsulated the Wallabies' triumph. They knew of the dangers lurking wide in the New Zealand three-quarter line. They were aware of the flair, the pace and the brilliance the All Blacks' backline possessed. They also knew that to kneecap the glamour boys, the possession lifeline had to be cut.

And so the Wallabies set about dismantling the New Zealand pack. The central targets were Collins and Mealamu. Jones circled them as the heartbeat of an All Blacks side that, once on the front foot, could demolish any opposition.

"They are their big go-forward forwards," he said.

"Some of their plays rely consistently on them taking the ball forward. So we had defenders in those areas to look after them. But from general play it was a team responsibility to shut them down."

Jones had been plotting for three months, since the All Blacks beat Australia 21-17 at Eden Park in Auckland in the Wallabies' last Test before RWC 2003. He believed he could formulate the strategy to bring down the Kiwis, but it required more than tactical nous.

Fitness would be another key element. The Wallabies were lacking it earlier in the season. Jones claims a shortage of gas held them back in that final Bledisloe Cup match – the game he used as his starting-point for the semi-final assault.

"There's no doubt about it," he said. "It was something we said all along. We were aiming to be at our fittest at this time of year and we worked very hard on it.

"We can't be fitter now. We're at our best. We've had a plan all year to get here in this condition. And what fitness allows you to do is execute without errors for longer periods of time.

"The match in Auckland showed us where we needed to attack and how we needed to attack. What we didn't do that day was execute well."

By stopping the go-forward Mealamu and Collins usually provided, the Wallabies nullified the effectiveness of Spencer and a lauded back three of Mils Muliaina, Doug Howlett and Joe Rokocoko.

But there were other primary targets too. The New Zealand lineout can be brittle. Australia won 50 percent of Kiwi throws in this year's Bledisloe Tests. The Wallabies again contested, with second-rower Justin Harrison a thorn in the All Blacks' side.

The Wallabies were also programmed to trust their attacking ability. Kicking the ball, unless absolutely necessary, was out. No free possessions for the NZ back three. At the same time, making inroads was crucial.

"What we were able to do was get good go-forward ourselves," said Jones. "Against New Zealand, you've got to hit the line hard. That's what our forwards did and the result was good ball.

"We also felt within their backline we could expose certain individuals if we executed well. But we had to go forward first. Playing with width doesn't just come from throwing the ball wide.

"It comes from going forward. We wanted to keep the ball in hand and attack them. In the end it was a real team effort. That was the thing. Everyone did their job."

And that included the coach who had drawn up the master-plan.

Game of two halves

The Gods of rugby, in pitting these two ancient European rivals together, had no doubt chosen the perfect match-up for an enthralling semi-final. The free-flowing passion of the French against the control and discipline of the English, Latin flair against Anglo-Saxon attention to detail ... this was also billed as a battle between two great schools of rugby thought and, after the steamy heat of the previous day's semi-final, everything pointed to an enthralling encounter.

But if France ever had a chance of winning this semi-final, it dissolved even before the kick-off on a stormy Sunday evening at Telstra Stadium. About two hours before the players came out onto the pitch, a violent tropical storm burst, seemingly right over the ground at Homebush.

Thunder and lightning quickly dampened the spirits of the fans, torrential rain saturated the field, and among the 82,346 spectators, there were many who instantly recalled France's ill-starred 1991 semi-final against South Africa in Durban, when another freak storm delayed the kick-off for several hours and the game was eventually played in cataclysmic conditions.

As it happened, the storm quickly abated, and although there was a 15°C temperature drop from the previous day's semi-final, the blustery wind even dried the pitch out to a certain extent before kick-off. But almost as soon as the game started, the conditions deteriorated yet again and as the game wore on, the gusty wind and driving rain were to become a dominant factor, playing into the English hands and nullifying the strengths of the French attack.

Never once did the French manage to dictate the terms of the encounter and with the English

pack applying enormous pressure in the tight phases, the much-vaunted French trio of loose forwards – Serge Betsen, Olivier Magne and Imanol Harinordoquy – did not have an impact on the game. Shackled by the slippery ball, sucked into the secondary combat phases by a juggernaut English pack intent on keeping the ball close to their chest, the French fliers were forced to stay close to the action, and to play the game not on their terms, but on the Englishmen's.

For the first 20 minutes, however, the game remained delicately poised with neither side gaining the upper hand. Jonny Wilkinson, who was to have another superlative night with the boot, kicking all 24 of his team's points from three field

BELOW 'Where do you think you're going?' England's Lawrence Dallaglio has free-running French counterpart Imanol Harinordoquy all tied up.

OPPOSITE Forward command post: once again England's pack was the solid foundation on which a comprehensive victory was built.

goals and five penalties, opened the scoring with a smartly-taken dropped goal in the ninth minute.

France replied almost immediately, however, with flanker Serge Betsen bolting over for a try from a lineout 25 metres out from the English line. Frédéric Michalak converted, to put France ahead 7-3, but these were to be the last points scored by the French as they gradually succumbed to the pressure of the English, who adapted far better to the conditions.

"We based our whole World Cup campaign on playing on hard grounds with a dry ball, and there is no question that we were handicapped by the rain," said French coach Bernard Laporte afterwards.

"But we are not going to use that as an excuse. The conditions were the same for both sides, and at this level of the competition you have to be able to adapt. England were more efficient, more intelligent, they adapted better to the conditions, and we have to congratulate them. We were just fragile in our fundamentals, and we made too many simple mistakes: we were not beaten by the rain, we were beaten by a better team, and that is what sport is all about."

As frustration began to build in the French camp, some of 'les Bleus' started to lose their nerve. Christophe Dominici was yellow-carded for a senseless foot-trip on Jason Robinson as the exciting English winger stepped inside him, and from the ensuing penalty, 43 metres out and five metres from the left-hand touchline, Wilkinson goaled to narrow the scores to 7-6. France were still in the game two minutes before half-time, but a second field goal to the English points machine, followed by another penalty, from 41 metres, saw the English go ahead 12-7 at the turn-around.

In the second half, with the rain sweeping even more relentlessly across the pitch, the English continued to strengthen their strangle-hold on the game. For a short period, Wilkinson began to imitate Michalak, missing two penalty attempts while the Frenchman missed one, but the turning-point came in the 54th minute when Betsen late-tackled Wilkinson in centre-field. Referee Paddy O'Brien had little choice but to show Betsen a yellow card.

The final quarter was all England, as Wilkinson goaled from the Betsen penalty, slotted a third field goal, and capped off another masterful performance with two more penalty goals.

ABOVE First capped against Argentina back in 1990, Jason Leonard came on at the start and finish of the semi-final to claim a world record 112th international cap. The Harlequins' prop, now 35, has made 107 England appearances, the other five coming with the Lions.

OPPOSITE Rien ne va plus: Fabien Galthié spent too much time under pressure to provide the quality ball his back-line needed. His English counterpart Matt Dawson, meanwhile, was revelling in the conditions with a match-winning performance of his own.

With England gradually gaining the upper hand in all sectors of play, even in the set scrums where France were expected to dominate, the French continued to muff the few chances they had. They dropped passes, knocked the ball on, and even five-eighth Michalak, who was billed as the up-and-coming French star after a faultless Rugby World Cup campaign, started to wilt under the pressure. He failed to ignite the back-line, his tactical kicking was disastrous, and his goalkicking eluded him, missing four penalties from a comfortable range before being replaced by Gérald Merceron after 64 minutes.

"It is in games like this that Jonny's real class shows," said England's captain Martin Johnson, pointing to Wilkinson's 'resurrection' after being lambasted in the press leading up to the semi-final.

"Michalak under pressure was making mistakes, but Jonny handled the situation brilliantly. He just kept us ticking over. Rugby is a simple game; it is all about getting go-forward. You win the ball, you go forward with it, and you play a good kicking game."

Johnson went on to explain that they used the same tactics as had allowed Australia to dominate New Zealand in the first semi-final the day before.

"We were confident that we could stop France from scoring," he said.

"We pressured their ball, and as the game wore on you could see them getting a little frustrated ...".

Finally, apart from the result, this semi-final also signalled two significant milestones in the history of the game. Jason Leonard, who came on to replace Phil Vickery for scarcely a minute at the very beginning of the match, and then returned to replace the other prop Trevor Woodman in the 79th minute, became the most-capped player in the history of international rugby, winning his 112th cap to surpass the great French centre Philippe Sella's previous record. And at 34 years old, and after playing in four Rugby World Cups, the French captain Fabien Galthié announced his retirement from the game at the end of the match.

As for England coach Clive Woodward, in his inimitable style, he took a parting shot at the French, dismissing the idea that the rain had handicapped them by preventing them from putting their game plan into action.

"I often go to France on holiday, and I can tell you that it rains a lot there," he said.

"The conditions were the conditions, and this game is all about winning. And even if the ground had been hard and the ball had been dry, we would have won."

BELOW Moment of truth: Christophe Dominici is about to be sin-binned for a trip on England's Jason Robinson. The Frenchman was hurt – and so were any chances his team had of rescuing the match.

OPPOSITE Point of difference: Wilkinson's ability to deal with the conditions, dropping three goals and converting five penalty kicks, was England's trump card on a night when English excellence beat French flair.

THIRD/FOURTH PLAYOFF

PLAYOFF RESULTS

NEW ZEALAND **40** d FRANCE **13**
Telstra Stadium, Sydney

Finishing flourish

The All Blacks finished their disappointing RWC 2003 campaign on a high, and with a fair bit of their trademark style, as they ran in six tries to beat France and clinch third place.

The playoff for third has a history of being a difficult assignment for everyone involved, as both teams have to pick themselves up quickly from the shock of a semi-final defeat.

Yet both New Zealand and France turned up to play at Sydney's Telstra Stadium, much to the delight of the 62,000 fans who turned out to watch.

There was a feeling throughout the tournament that the All Blacks and Tricolores were the best attacking teams. In the semi-finals they had been out-thought and out-muscled by the huge defences of Australia and England respectively.

On a balmy Thursday evening, they brought almost a Barbarians approach to the playoff. The result was seven tries in a contest that was a close affair deep into the match. The All Blacks led only 14-13 early in the second half, but two quick tries ripped France apart and set New Zealand on their way to a consolation prize.

Having entered the tournament as one of the favourites and with the world No.1 ranking swinging between them and England throughout the event, third place was little comfort. But they were determined to finish with a bit of flair, and left knowing third is way better than fourth in the minds of their hard-nosed fans and critics.

The All Blacks finished the tournament with a Rugby World Cup-record 52 tries and had the deadly duo of Doug Howlett and Mils Muliaina on top of the individual list with seven tries each. One try back was Joe Rokocoko on six, as all three backs scored against France.

Rokocoko's effort took his season tally to 17, extending his New Zealand record and equalling the world record for tries in one year.

All Blacks coach John Mitchell spoke highly of that, and it was a strong message at the business end of the tournament when the differing philosophies of the game of rugby were imprinted on RWC 2003.

"I believe we have scored 81 tries in 2003 – 40 of them by the wingers. I think it's a wonderful way to play rugby and though we came unstuck last weekend, in many ways those opportunities still existed in the first 15 minutes [against Australia] ... we just didn't put them away."

Mitchell felt the win over France proved the spirit in his squad.

"It's been a difficult week for all of us, but the whole group has been outstanding. In a short turnaround to get up and get a result – and a convincing result – is a credit to everyone."

Playmaker Carlos Spencer, with a pack firing in front of him and giving him plenty of ball to work with, orchestrated the All Blacks' attack magnificently. He backed up Mitchell's comments as the All Blacks headed home, still searching for their first Rugby World Cup title 16 years after winning the inaugural event in 1987.

"We had one hiccup last week and that cost us big time, but I think we can hold our heads high," said Spencer. "The coaches gave the starting fifteen another chance, and we went out there and did that."

OPPOSITE Thanks for the memories: Doug Howlett and the All Blacks acknowledge the crowd's support after clinching third place.

PREVIOUS PAGE Slipping away: New Zealand's Joe Rokocoko evades a lunging French defender as he runs in his seventh try of the tournament.

Spencer felt it was a good way to end what he believed was a good season despite the major hiccup last Saturday.

"I think people have to realise that you just can't look at last week as our season. It would have been nice to get the World Cup and put it alongside the Bledisloe and Tri-Nations. But we have to put that behind us. We are a young team and I think we can only get better."

Spencer admitted he felt it hard to pick himself up from the disappointment of the loss to Australia. "I can't speak for everyone, but personally I felt it

hard to build up for this. But each individual did their job despite the short turnaround."

New Zealand captain Reuben Thorne was delighted with the way his players responded.

"I'm very happy with the way the guys picked themselves up. We had no choice but to move on from what was a pretty shattering event," said Thorne. "We got some good tries and showed that we wanted to play with the ball tonight. It's been a long, hard year, and it's been draining physically and emotionally, especially the last week. We didn't get what we wanted here, but the guys have all

grown and I think the tournament has been great for rugby."

French coach Bernard Laporte lamented his side's inability to take their chances just after half-time. They had scored a quick try to get back to within one point and were hot on the attack. Yet, they turned the ball over, and the All Blacks counter-attack resulted in Rokocoko's try. Brad Thorn touched down a couple of minutes later out of a quick lineout and it was all over for the French as the All Blacks picked up the pace.

"That was the telling time for us," said Laporte.

"It was a disappointing end for us but I think France can be proud of their World Cup."

France has featured heavily in all five tournaments, yet is still seeking its first Webb Ellis Cup.

The two teams took different approaches to this match. The All Blacks put 14 of the players who lost to Australia out again to atone for that disappointment. Laporte opted for fresh legs and minds, making 13 changes to the side that failed to take on England.

Mitchell's gamble on his players digging deep paid off. There was certainly plenty of attitude and enthusiasm from the All Blacks, even if the fluency wasn't always there. But this was a game the All Blacks always controlled. It was just a pity the attitude wasn't there five days earlier.

Now New Zealand and France must wait another four years. They left an imprint for attacking rugby on RWC 2003, but they need to mix a bit of fortitude into that recipe for their next assault.

FINAL

FINAL RESULT

ENGLAND **20** d AUSTRALIA **17**
Telstra Stadium, Sydney

A fitting finale

The world of rugby held its breath for a heartbeat as Matt Dawson's pass sped towards England fly-half Jonny Wilkinson. He was poised just outside Australia's 22, a shade to the left of the posts, and every person in the crowd of 82,957 at Telstra Stadium and in the global television audience knew what was coming next. But could the most talked-about rugby player on the planet deliver?

The game had tipped over into the 100th minute of play and Australia was still clinging doggedly to the hope of claiming the William Webb Ellis Cup for a third time; the bullocking English had driven play, but Australia's game rodeo rider had so far refused to be thrown.

Elton Flatley twice hauled the Wallabies back into the saddle with cool-as-you-like penalties – one in the 80th minute to take the game into extra time, and then another in the 99th minute to put his side level once more, which threatened the possibility of 10 minutes of sudden-death extra time.

The decisive moment of the tournament had arrived – 64 hours and 20 minutes of playing time after the opening whistle 43 days earlier on the same ground.

Could Wilkinson deliver rugby's Holy Grail into England's hands and wrest it away from those of the Southern Hemisphere for the first time in 16 years?

He'd already tried and failed with three drop goal attempts and a fourth by teammate Mike Catt had been charged down. But now there was time and space – lots of time, in fact, because sporting immortality was beckoning.

Wilkinson's strike with his right foot – not his natural side – was perfect and the ball sailed through the uprights to put England into the lead for a third and final time.

Australia had less than 30 seconds to produce another miracle, but England secured possession from the restart and it fell to Catt to end Rugby World Cup 2003 with a thumping clearance kick into touch.

Those final two minutes had summed up England's tournament, hallmarked by composure, competence, massive self-confidence and, of course, extraordinary talent.

Following Flatley's 99th-minute leveller, England worked its way into position for the winning drop goal with the precision of a chess grandmaster.

First, it kicked the restart long to force Australia to clear the terrestrial danger to touch. Then, it won the lineout and drove the ball to the posts through Catt in the centres.

Australia read the danger and was poised to charge Wilkinson as he dropped back into the pocket, but Dawson took advantage by darting through the defence close to the ruck to steal another 10 metres.

Wilkinson was now perfectly positioned for his drop attempt, but with his scrum-half buried at the bottom of the ruck, England captain Martin Johnson stood off and called to auxiliary halfback Neil Back to give him the ball.

The lock forward thundered back to the point from which he had received it, allowing time for Dawson to bob back into position. Again the Wallabies were poised, but the 57-cap scrum-half delayed his pass until the defenders had been forced to retire behind the last feet of the ruck to give

OPPOSITE Six minutes into the final, Australia's Lote Tuqiri uses his height to full advantage to beat Jason Robinson and score his country's try.

BELOW Robinson's revenge: with 38 minutes on the clock the England winger replies with a sliding try into the left-hand corner.

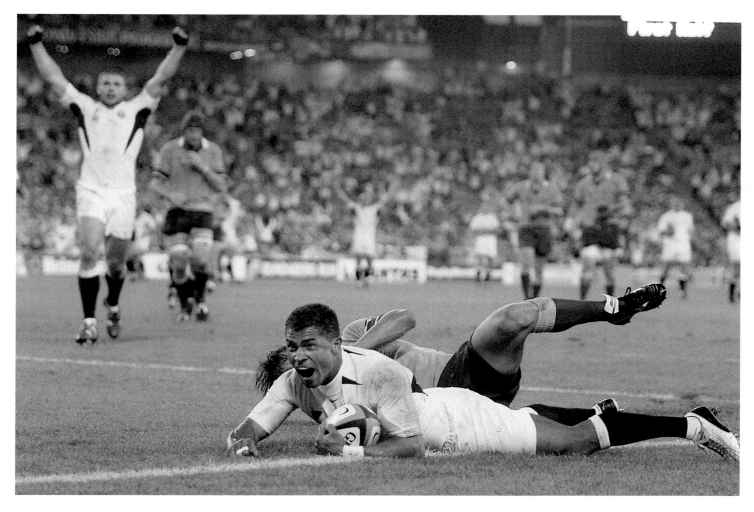

Wilkinson more than enough time to deliver to England not just the Rugby World Cup, but that country's first global sporting title since the soccer World Cup was won 37 years before.

"When they kicked the penalty we called the long kick-off," said Johnson. "They put it into touch and we called the lineout as well and pretty much wanted to take it straight up the middle and keep going at them.

"Once Matt had made the break through the middle, I just took it up once more – I'm glad I caught it – and there were 30 seconds, 20 seconds to go and Wilko in front of the sticks to win the World Cup.

"I'm sure he's been through that scenario a few times on the training field and I'm sure you wouldn't want anyone else there, would you? It was a case then of catching the ball from the kick-off and then kicking it out – it was just about the only bit of play that went to plan!"

Wallaby coach Eddie Jones said: "They set up the field goal very well. You have got to admire the control that they had. Was it inevitable? If we had pulled off a good tackle and put a bit more of a fast defensive set on, we could have put a bit of pressure on Wilkinson, but they played those last minutes very well, which again just shows that they are a class outfit to win those close games.

"Champion sides win close games – that's what they did."

It was a monumental effort, too, from the Wallabies. They perfectly executed a training ground plan to take the lead in the sixth minute when fly-half Stephen Larkham's right-to-left perfect hanging bomb came down on England's goal line and into the hands of wing Lote Tuqiri, who exploited his 9cm height advantage over marker Jason Robinson.

Flatley struck the near upright with the touchline conversion attempt into the curtain of light drizzle that periodically doused the game. England then used the wind at its back to take what appeared to be a game-breaking lead of nine points into half-time.

BELOW How much did Stephen Larkham's absence hurt Australia? The inspirational fly-half spent 28 of the game's 100 minutes in the blood bin.

OPPOSITE Courage under pressure: Elton Flatley's nerveless kicking clawed Australia back into the contest, both at the end of 80 minutes and again at the close of extra time.

LEFT For England coach Clive Woodward, celebrating with match-winner Wilkinson, Sydney 2003 was the culmination of a six-year campaign to drive England relentlessly to the top.

OPPOSITE The final turning-point of RWC 2003 – and what more fitting finale than a Wilkinson drop goal to claim the Webb Ellis Trophy?

Wilkinson landed three penalties in 14 minutes – the first two a bare handful of metres in Australian territory – before England completed the half with a sweet try of their own.

From a lineout on the right, centre Will Greenwood drove the ball to just beyond the Wallaby 10-metre line and possession was quickly recycled for England's No.8, Lawrence Dallaglio, to come swooping down the blindside left.

He was taken round the ankles but passed as he fell to Wilkinson supporting on his inside. The fly-half flicked the ball back to the left to the overlapping Robinson. The winger was uncatchable from 20 metres and made sure by diving short of the line to slither in at the left corner flag.

But that was England's last score until the second minute of extra-time as the Wallabies' superior discipline helped them claw their way back into the game. Three penalties from four attempts by Flatley punished an increasingly perplexed England on those occasions the Wallabies were able to break out of their own half. England was perplexed because although it kept finding good field position, the scoreboard refused to budge.

"We just never got a grip of it in the second half," said Johnson. "We'd get down there and make silly

ABOVE Find someone to hug, or find somewhere to hide...

OPPOSITE TOP English and proud of it: outstanding No.8 Lawrence Dallaglio proudly wears his winner's medal.

OPPOSITE BOTTOM Another way of saying the same thing: England centre Will Greenwood welcomes the moment a great rugby nation has been waiting for.

mistakes. At one stage both sides were winning each other's lineouts – at one stage we won three of theirs and they won three of ours – so you couldn't get any pattern on the game.

"We made so many silly errors – we didn't score a point in the second half which is unlike us because once we've got ahead, if we'd got into position, Jonny would have kicked us three, six, nine points to win us the game. If we had lost that game, I don't know what we'd have done with ourselves, because it was there to be won."

That's what the Wallabies thought too when Flatley's third penalty, from the 22 just to the right of the posts, sailed through the uprights in the 80th minute after England conceded one of the five penalties it gave away at what had been a dominant scrum throughout the tournament. Having led for

an hour and with the Webb Ellis Cup 30 seconds from its reach, this was England's real test.

Wilkinson helped it rise to it. He nervelessly slotted another 47-metre penalty two minutes into the first period of extra-time to bolster morale.

And there the game stood for another 15 minutes – either side of missed drop goal attempts by Catt and Wilkinson – until Flatley once again stilled a beating heart to throw Australia that 99th-minute lifeline.

It was sporting drama paced to perfection. Its author, however, turned out to be English rather than Australian as Wilkinson followed South Africa's Joel Stransky into history by winning a Rugby World Cup with an extra-time drop goal.

"You slug it out over 100 minutes and you get beaten in the 99th minute – I think that would

qualify as a photo-finish," said Australia's Eddie Jones. "Although we've come up short the players have given everything they can. This side has showed tremendous resolve – it's a side that the country should be enormously proud of. We went down with all guns blazing."

England's Clive Woodward said: "Between the two of us we conspired to produce a pretty epic final. Well done to Australia; they were outstanding against the All Blacks (in the semi-final) and really stepped up to the mark against us.

"We made a lot of errors and kept letting them back into the game, but I think we deserved to win. But we're going home with a win and lasting memories of this match and the atmosphere that was just fantastic. What happened on the pitch at the end will live with us forever."

THROUGH THE LENS

Hope and triumph, defeat and despair. One man's magic against a team's sheer grit. Flying tackles, jinking runs. Tries scored, tears shed. And through it all, the memories of a lifetime: RWC 2003 through the lens...

TOP LEFT All angles covered: France's Frédéric Michalak was in brilliant form with the boot early on, adding the edge to his side's attacking play.

BOTTOM LEFT Joe Rokocoko of New Zealand redefines the term "flying winger" with the first of the All Blacks' eight tries against Wales.

ABOVE Lengthening shadows, gathering gloom: Nicky Little cuts a lonely figure as he realises Fiji's World Cup is over, beaten 22-20 by the Scots in the Sydney sun.

127

LEFT No cause for concern: Greg Somerville and his New Zealand teammates check the big screen during the 91-7 defeat of Tonga in Brisbane.

TOP 'I know I'm supposed to fit in here somewhere': the England maul gets up close and personal against Uruguay at Suncorp Stadium.

ABOVE No wonder Juan Menchaca wants to party with the Aussie Stadium fans: Uruguay are enjoying their solitary victory, 24-12 against Georgia.

LEFT Rallying round the flag: the Wallabies form a tight-knit group as they await their National Anthem before the Pool A match against Romania at Suncorp Stadium.

BOTTOM LEFT On his way homeward: Kenny Logan of Scotland, in his last Rugby World Cup, can't hold back the tears after losing the Brisbane quarter-final to Australia 33-16.

BELOW The City of Churches finds a new religion as Paul O'Connell of Ireland rises high to win lineout ball against Argentina at Adelaide Oval.

ABOVE LEFT Good evening! Carl Hoeft of New Zealand prepares to give his Tongan counterpart a warm welcome in the Pool D match at Suncorp Stadium.

TOP 'Are you ready? Pull!' England's Dan Luger (left) and Martin Corry make life difficult for Uruguay flanker Nicolas Brignoni in their Pool C match on November 2.

ABOVE 'You can't catch me!' Shin Hasegawa's despairing dive is not enough to stop high-stepping Frenchman Damien Traille during the Pool B match in Townsville which France won 51-29.

LEFT Gonzalo Canale of Italy demonstrates balletic poise as he offloads during the Pool D match with Tonga at Canberra Stadium.

TOP 'How good is that?' Tongan centre Pierre Hola shows his delight at scoring his side's only try against the mighty All Blacks in their Pool D encounter.

ABOVE It's mine: Ireland's Kevin Maggs pounces on a loose ball during the rain-soaked encounter against Namibia at Sydney's Aussie Stadium.

Zinzan Brooke's

Team of the tournament

Perhaps the greatest No.8 in the history of the game, former New Zealand captain Zinzan Brooke was a member of his country's 1987 Rugby World Cup-winning squad. He played 58 Tests for the All Blacks from 1987-1997, scored a world record 17 Test tries for a forward and could also drop match-winning goals. Few know more about performing on rugby's biggest stage, and few could argue with any of the RWC 2003 superstars selected in his team of the tournament. The 22-man squad profiled in the following pages is a team cast in the mould of Zinzan himself: a thoughtful blend of exuberant flair and battle-hardened experience, a winning mixture of strength and skill.

1. Loosehead prop
BILL YOUNG
Australia

Club: Eastwood
Born: March 4, 1975
Height: 188cm
Weight: 110kg
Caps: 25

RWC 2003
Matches: 6
Tries: 0
Points: 0

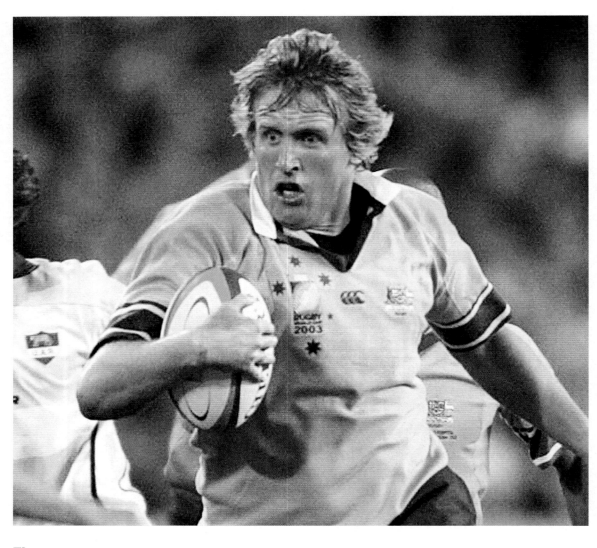

Zinzan says:

Bill doesn't look like a prop – he looks more like a gunslinger, and he hasn't got a big physique compared to others at 188cm and 110kg. But his work rate around the field is outstanding, and he pops up everywhere in defence and attack. He's also very clever at scrum time and can often negate the opponents' weight advantage with experience and technique. He's a very unassuming player and he's often not in the limelight, but consistently he remains one of the best props in world rugby and he's been around a while. A vital cog in the Wallaby team and one of the reasons for its success at RWC 2003.

2. Hooker
KEVEN MEALAMU
New Zealand

Club: Otahuhu
Born: March 20, 1979
Height: 181cm
Weight: 106kg
Caps: 13

RWC 2003
Matches: 5
Tries: 1
Points: 5

Zinzan says:

This position was a close call. Brendan Cannon had a great game against the All Blacks and probably shaded Mealamu on that day, but I didn't think he was that impressive in other matches. Also, Keith Wood is a superb player, but Ireland got knocked out in the quarters so that works against him, although I've got Wood on the bench. Throughout the tournament, I think Mealamu was the pick of the hookers. His tackle and ball-carrying ability was superb, and, although his lineout work came under pressure in the loss to Australia in the semis, it was pretty strong overall. Also, from a hooking point of view, his scrummaging is strong, and he's just 24, so he'll come through even more. What I like best about Mealamu is the confrontation game he plays in close quarters. He has an uncanny knack of breaking the gain line, as he did against South Africa in the quarters in Melbourne where he scored a superb try to give New Zealand the winning lead.

3. Tighthead Prop
PHIL VICKERY
England

Club: Gloucester
Born: March 14, 1976
Height: 191cm
Weight: 125kg
Caps: 38

RWC 2003
Matches: 7
Tries: 1
Points: 5

Zinzan says:

I don't think we saw the best of Vickery in the tournament, but I like his bulk (he weighs 125kg and he's 191cm tall), and the way he anchors the England scrum is superb. He's only 27, still quite young for a prop, which means he'll probably get better. I also like his work rate around the field and he's a very skilful player. He took his try against Samoa well and has a positive attitude about the game, which is important. He seems to really enjoy his rugby, which I also like, and he combines well with the other English forwards in rolling mauls, an important part of the game for England.

4. Lock
MARTIN JOHNSON
England

Club: Leicester
Born: March 9, 1970
Height: 200cm
Weight: 118kg
Caps: 84

RWC 2003
Matches: 7
Tries: 1
Points: 5

Zinzan says:

Not too much doubt about this one. Johnson is such a good leader he's my natural pick as captain, and his domination at the front of the lineout gives England a constant supply of ball. His work in setting up and driving the England rolling maul was a key to their success, and he has an incredibly high work rate in both defence and attack. For such a big guy, his skills are impressive, and he has a "never say die, never panic" attitude. England came from behind to beat Samoa, then Wales in the quarters and France in the semis – that says a lot for Johnson's leadership. He has the utmost respect of every player in his team as well as most of the opposition, which is vital if you want to be a successful leader.

5. Lock
CHRIS JACK
New Zealand

Club: Shirley
Born: September 5, 1978
Height: 202cm
Weight: 112kg
Caps: 25

RWC 2003
Matches: 5
Tries: 1
Points: 5

Zinzan says:

This was a tough decision, with Ben Kay of England and Bakkies Botha from South Africa both pushing hard, but in the end, I went for Jack. As well as being a good back-of-the-lineout jumper, he's very mobile and his athleticism and work rate are outstanding. His work on the fringes and in the ruck and maul is also good, and I liked the way he finished off strongly against France. He could've chucked in the towel after the semi-final disappointment against Australia, but he kept going right to the end and played well as New Zealand claimed third place.

6. Blindside Flanker
GEORGE SMITH
Australia

Club: Manly
Born: July 17, 1980
Height: 180cm
Weight: 98kg
Caps: 35

RWC 2003
Matches: 7
Tries: 2
Points: 10

Zinzan says:

I would've liked to go for Richard Hill here, but I can't as injury meant he really didn't play enough. Smith had one of the toughest jobs in this Rugby World Cup as he's used to playing openside flanker. When the Wallabies started to play Phil Waugh there, he had to adapt quickly to blindside. I think he found himself a little out in the wilderness at first, but he's taken it on board and adapted brilliantly, really making the position his own. Smith also has the ability to step up at the big games, like in the semi-final against the All Blacks where he certainly dominated – and that was up against Richie McCaw, which is no mean feat.

7. Openside flanker
RICHIE McCAW
New Zealand

Club: Christchurch

Born: December 31, 1980

Height: 188cm

Weight: 105kg

Caps: 21

RWC 2003

Matches: 7

Tries: 0

Points: 0

Zinzan says:

For me, there's no doubt about this one. Richie is the complete loose forward, and during RWC 2003 he was just brilliant. He's really solid in every aspect of his game – competing for the ball at the breakdown, supporting after a break or taking the ball up himself. There's nothing he can't do. The only time he was nullified to an extent during the tournament was against Australia where the Wallabies double-teamed him, putting up both George Smith and Phil Waugh against him. He still performed capably against two players. He's just 22, so he'll be only 26 at the next RWC. To me, he'll be the next All Black captain.

8. No.8
LAWRENCE DALLAGLIO
England

Club: Wasps
Born: August 10, 1972
Height: 193cm
Weight: 109kg
Caps: 65

RWC 2003
Matches: 7
Tries: 1
Points: 5

Zinzan says:

This is a tough one as there were a lot of contenders, but I don't think that anyone really did enough to take the spot away from Dallaglio. He's a 31-year-old and he gets a lot of "Dad's Army" taunts, but if you look at his all-round play at this World Cup, it's been superb – and much better than a lot of younger players'. In a lot of games, he really stamped his mark, especially when Richard Hill was out injured and England had a combination of Neil Back and Lewis Moody as flankers, which I don't think worked too well. Dallaglio had to carry a lot of the load and I think he rose to the challenge pretty well. He can be a bloody nuisance to sides that he's playing against because he gets in and does a lot of good work at the breakdown. He had a fantastic tour to New Zealand and Australia in June and I think he carried that right through the Rugby World Cup. He's played outstandingly well and answered his critics.

9. Scrum-half
JUSTIN MARSHALL
New Zealand

Club: Sumner
Born: August 8, 1973
Height: 179cm
Weight: 94kg
Caps: 70

RWC 2003
Matches: 5
Tries: 1
Points: 5

Zinzan says:

His all-round game during the tournament was first-class. At times, he was like another loose forward for the All Blacks, and he added so much to the New Zealand team around the fringes, making a run or pulling off a big tackle. His big hit on the South African prop in the quarter-final in Melbourne really sticks in the mind in what was probably the All Blacks' best performance in the tournament. He has a solid pass rather than a great one, but all his other attributes in RWC 2003 were outstanding. Against Wales in the Pool D game, he was just awesome. Justin also took on a real leadership role within the team, and it made a big difference when he had to be replaced in the semi-final against Australia. The moment he was injured may have been the moment when the All Blacks were knocked out of RWC 2003. This tournament was probably his last Rugby World Cup, and he went out on a high note.

10. Fly-half
JONNY WILKINSON
England

Club: Newcastle
Born: May 25, 1979
Height: 178cm
Weight: 89kg
Caps: 52

RWC 2003
Matches: 6
Tries: 0
Cons: 10
Pens: 23
DG: 8
Points: 113

Zinzan says:

This was a tough decision. If New Zealand had got through to the final, I might've gone for Carlos Spencer, but in the end, you can't go past Wilkinson. A lot of people jumped on his case, especially after the game against Wales, but to me, he's the all-round complete player. His kicking ability is just first-class, and in the big matches, you need to know that your fly-half can slot the goals when required. He has an old head on young shoulders, and out on the field he seems so cool and focused. He knows what to do at almost every moment. Another thing about Wilkinson, which is perhaps unusual for a fly-half, is that he's very solid in defence. He also likes to get involved in the rucks and, mauls and maybe does that a little too much as the fly-half has to be ready when an opportunity arises. But he likes that physical aspect, and isn't scared of contact.

11. Left wing
RUPENI CAUCAU
Fiji

Club: Auckland
Born: June 5, 1980
Height: 175cm
Weight: 98kg
Caps: 4

RWC 2003
Matches: 2
Tries: 3
Points: 15

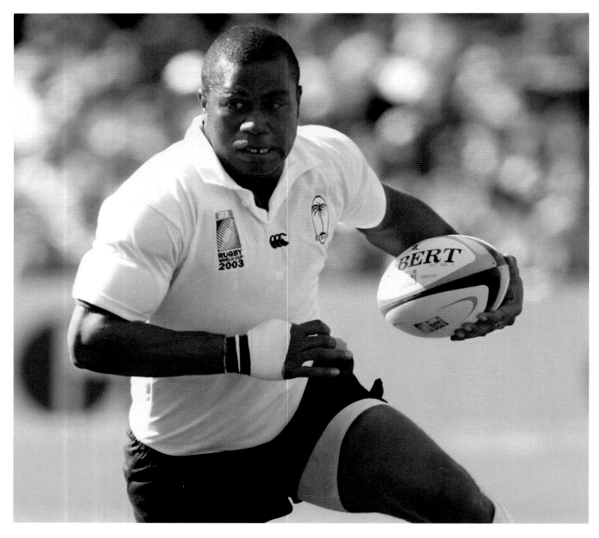

Zinzan says:

My only complaint about Rupeni is that we didn't see him enough. But although he only played two games due to missing another two through suspension, I saw him enough to give him my left-wing spot. Caucau is just quality, and one of the most exciting players on the planet. There's not enough words to describe him. He's fantastic on his feet, great with ball in hand, and a great advertisement for what's best about rugby. For me, one of the moments of the tournament was Caucau against France. He had hardly any room but he ran around Aurélien Rougerie – a great winger himself – in the space of five metres. His two tries in the first half against Scotland were just as incredible, and aged just 23, I think he'll be thrilling rugby crowds for many years to come.

12. Inside Centre
BRIAN LIMA
Samoa

Club: Secom
Born: January 25, 1972
Height: 181cm
Weight: 95kg
Caps: 54

RWC 2003
Matches: 4
Tries: 3
Points: 15

Zinzan says:

In the centres I've gone for the two Brians – O'Driscoll and Lima. Brian Lima is known as "The Chiropractor" because he's renowned for his fearsome tackles. But it's not just his defence that is outstanding. At 34, he was playing in his fourth Rugby World Cup, and his contribution was huge. He played outstandingly well. Excellent in attack, he created a really solid base in the midfield that was very important for Samoa. Brian has the ability to take it up or, as I noted earlier, make a big tackle that will send his opponents back. I like this combination of the two Brians together. O'Driscoll has flair, while Lima is solid. Lima could make the half-break to put O'Driscoll through or take the pressure off his outside centre with a few strong runs that would give O'Driscoll more room to manoeuvre.

13. Outside Centre
BRIAN O'DRISCOLL
Ireland

Club: Blackrock
Born: January 21, 1979
Height: 180cm
Weight: 94kg
Caps: 46

RWC 2003
Matches: 5
Tries: 3
DG: 1
Points: 18

Zinzan says:

Brian is a very well-balanced player, and he has tremendous skills. That's not just with the ball in hand or splitting opposition defences as we've all seen him do again and again. He's also very good at the ruck and maul, which is not the case with all backs. He knows how to get in and recover the ball for his team and is not scared of contact. One moment that summed up Brian for me was against France in the quarter-final in Melbourne. Tony Marsh, the French centre, had made a break and was charging for the line when O'Driscoll got back in cover defence and cut him down. Then, like a loose forward, he was on his feet in a split second, ripping the ball from Marsh and getting Ireland out of a tricky situation. He has incredible ability, and at only 24, I think he's just going to get better. I don't think we saw the best of him at RWC 2003, although he was among Ireland's best against France.

14. Right wing
DOUG HOWLETT
New Zealand

Club: Marist Auckland
Born: September 21, 1978
Height: 185cm
Weight: 92kg
Caps: 38

RWC 2003
Matches: 7
Tries: 7
Points: 35

Zinzan says:

Like teammate Mils Muliaina, Doug scored seven tries, and showed during the tournament that he is one of the best finishers in world rugby. He runs nice angles and knows instinctively when to change his lines. Throughout RWC 2003, he constantly broke the opposition's defence because he knew when and where to run at them. He also knew when to come off his line in support and when to stay on it. Another thing about Dougie is that he's a great worker. He keeps going for the full 80 minutes and keeps getting involved, constantly inspiring his team or giving them some good go-forward with a strong run.

15. Fullback
MILS MULIAINA
New Zealand

Club: Suburbs
Born: July 31, 1980
Height: 183cm
Weight: 94kg
Caps: 14

RWC 2003
Matches: 7
Tries: 7
Points: 35

Zinzan says:

The equal top try-scorer in the tournament (along with Doug Howlett) with seven tries, Mils is a complete player. He has a good attacking game, is good on his feet and he knows when to run and when to kick. All round, he's a quality player. With Howlett and Joe Rokocoko, he formed the most dangerous back three in the tournament, and if you kicked badly to them you were in trouble. The only game where he really failed to make a massive impact was against Australia in the semi-final, and I think that was due to good Australian defence rather than any fault on his part. At just 23, he is a massive prospect for the future and could be a key player for the All Blacks for many years yet.

Coach
BERNARD LAPORTE
France

Country: France
Born: July 1, 1964

Six Nations and Grand Slam-winning coach 2002

Zinzan says:

This may surprise a few people, as France finished out of the major placings and some people are calling for his head. But I really like what he's done with this French team and how he's got them playing. He's improved their discipline incredibly, got them back on track and being competitive. Apart from the second half against the All Blacks in the playoff for third place, they were superb throughout the tournament. I also like his attitude to the game and the style of rugby he tries to play. France's first-half performance against Ireland was probably the best in the tournament and if fly-half Frederic Michalak had not missed some vital penalties against England at a crucial stage in the semi-final, they might have gone on to win the Rugby World Cup.

The bench

On the bench, I've gone for a mix of experience and good impact players.

16. Reserve Hooker KEITH WOOD
Ireland

Club: Garryowen
Born: January 27, 1972
Height: 183cm
Weight: 105kg
Caps: 58

RWC 2003
Matches: 5
Tries: 1
Points: 5

Zinzan says:
Keith Wood just missed out on the starting spot at hooker and has the coolness to come on late in the game and guide the team home

17. Reserve Prop KEES MEEUWS
New Zealand

Club: Waitakere
Born: July 26, 1974
Height: 183cm
Weight: 118kg
Caps: 35

RWC 2003
Matches: 6
Tries: 2
Points: 10

Zinzan says:
Kees Meeuws at prop is a very explosive player, and can be devastating at both scrum time and in open play. Look at the number of tries New Zealand scored when he's come on late in the game and given the All-Black scrum a real boost or powered his way over from close to the line.

18. Reserve Lock DAVID GIFFIN
Australia

Club: Sunnybank
Born: November 6, 1973
Height: 198cm
Weight: 115kg
Caps: 50

RWC 2003
Matches: 5
Tries: 0
Points: 0

Zinzan says:
David Giffin is another experienced player who has the ability to get up for the big games, and he's a very reliable lineout jumper, which is vital for winning secure ball at the end of the match. Australia used him off the bench in the last two games very effectively, and he made a real difference when he came on in the second half against New Zealand in the semi-final.

19.
Reserve Backrower
OLIVIER MAGNE

France

Club: Montferrand
Born: April 11, 1973
Height: 188cm
Weight: 95kg
Caps: 72

RWC 2003
Matches: 6
Tries: 1
Points: 5

Zinzan says:

Olivier Magne is another experienced player who, although he's turned 30, has everything. He's still got the whole package.

20.
Reserve Scrum-half
KYRAN BRACKEN

England

Club: Saracens
Born: November 22, 1971
Height: 180cm
Weight: 84kg
Caps: 51

RWC 2003
Matches: 4
Tries: 0
Points: 0

Zinzan says:

Kyran Bracken's my reserve scrum-half because I've been really impressed with what he's done when he's come on late in the game for England. He's snaffled out a lot of ball and really put the opposition's combinations under a lot of pressure. He could also do the same role from the start if required.

21.
Reserve Fly-half/ Fullback
STEPHEN LARKHAM

Australia

Club: ACT
Born: May 29, 1974
Height: 188cm
Weight: 86kg
Caps: 65

RWC 2003
Matches: 6
Tries: 2
Points: 10

Zinzan says:

You can't rule out Stephen Larkham, even if some people might like to. He has this incredible knack of pulling a rabbit out of his hat just when you've written him off completely. He's the sort of player who produces when he really needs to and can also slot in at fullback.

22.
Reserve Wing/ Centre
LOTE TUQIRI

Australia

Club: West Harbour
Born: September 23, 1979
Height: 191cm
Weight: 103kg
Caps: 14

RWC 2003
Matches: 7
Tries: 5
Points: 25

Zinzan says:

Lote Tuqiri was a revelation of this Rugby World Cup, and ever since the Namibian game, I was suggesting he should be in the starting line-up rather than Wendell Sailor. For me, Tuqiri is a lot more balanced player than Wendell – he's got a lot more movement, and late in the game if my team has a problem at blindside flanker, we can slot him in there.

Match synopsis and statistics

MATCH 1 POOL A

Joe Roff of Australia in action against Argentina.

AUSTRALIA 24 ARGENTINA 8
Telstra Stadium, October 10
Crowd: 81,350
Referee: Paul Honiss
Touch judges: Tony Spreadbury, Iain Ramage

AUSTRALIA
15	Mat Rogers
14	Wendell Sailor
13	Matthew Burke
12	Elton Flatley
11	Joe Roff (Lote Tuqiri, 78)
10	Stephen Larkham (Matt Giteau, 69)
9	George Gregan (captain) (Chris Whitaker, 77)
8	David Lyons
7	Phil Waugh
6	George Smith (Matt Cockbain, 68)
5	Nathan Sharpe
4	David Giffin (Daniel Vickerman, 41)
3	Al Baxter (Ben Darwin, 67)
2	Brendan Cannon (Jeremy Paul, 73)
1	Bill Young

Tries: Sailor, Roff
Con: Flatley
Pens: Flatley 4

ARGENTINA
15	Ignacio Corleto (Juan Martin Hernandez, 58-60)
14	Jose Maria Nunez Piossek
13	Manuel Contepomi
12	Jose Orengo
11	Diego Albanese
10	Felipe Contepomi
9	Agustin Pichot (captain)
8	Gonzalo Longo
7	Rolando Martin
6	Santiago Phelan (Martin Durand, 70)
5	Patricio Albacete
4	Ignacio Fernández Lobbe
3	Omar Hasan
2	Mario Ledesma
1	Roberto Grau (Mauricio Reggiardo, 67)

Unused replacements
16	Federico Mendez
18	Rimas Alvarez
20	Nicolas Fernandez Miranda
21	Gonzalo Quesada

Try: Corleto
Pen: F. Contepomi
Yellow card: M. Contepomi (23-33)

MATCH 2 POOL D

All Black Daniel Carter.

NEW ZEALAND 70 ITALY 7
Telstra Dome, October 11
Crowd: 40,715
Referee: Andrew Cole
Touch judges: Andre Watson, George Ayoub

NEW ZEALAND
15	Mils Muliaina
14	Doug Howlett
13	Tana Umaga (Ma'a Nonu, 24)
12	Daniel Carter
11	Joe Rokocoko (Leon MacDonald, 70)
10	Carlos Spencer
9	Justin Marshall
8	Jerry Collins (Rodney So'oialo, 66)
7	Richie McCaw (Marty Holah, 67)
6	Reuben Thorne (captain)
5	Chris Jack
4	Brad Thorn
3	Greg Somerville
2	Keven Mealamu (Mark Hammett, 63)
1	Dave Hewett (Kees Meeuws, 63)

Unused replacement
20	Steve Devine

Tries: Howlett 2, Spencer 2, Rokocoko 2, Thorn, Thorne, Carter, MacDonald, Marshall
Cons: Carter 6
Pens: Spencer

ITALY
15	Gert Peens
14	Mirco Bergamasco
13	Andrea Masi
12	Matteo Barbini
11	Nicola Mazzucato (Gonzalo Canale, 65)
10	Francesco Mazzariol
9	Matteo Mazzantini (Alessandro Troncon, 62)
8	Matthew Phillips (Andrea Benatti, 62)
7	Mauro Bergamasco (Sergio Parisse, 62)
6	Scott Palmer
5	Christian Bezzi
4	Carlo Checchinato (captain)
3	Ramiro Martinez (Martin Castrogiovanni, 65)
2	Carlo Festuccia (Fabio Ongaro, 17-22, 75)
1	Salvatore Perugini

Unused replacement
21	Rima Wakarua-Noema

Try: Phillips
Con: Peens

MATCH 3 POOL A

Ireland's star centre Brian O'Driscoll.

IRELAND 45 ROMANIA 17
Central Coast Stadium, October 11
Crowd: 19,193
Referee: Jonathan Kaplan
Touch judges: Tony Spreadbury, Iain Ramage

IRELAND
15	Girvan Dempsey
14	Shane Horgan
13	Brian O'Driscoll (John Kelly, 78)
12	Kevin Maggs
11	Denis Hickie
10	David Humphreys (Ronan O'Gara, 67)
9	Peter Stringer (Guy Easterby, 70)
8	Anthony Foley (Alan Quinlan, 55)
7	Keith Gleeson (Donnacha O'Callaghan, 77-80)
6	Victor Costello
5	Paul O'Connell
4	Malcolm O'Kelly
3	Reggie Corrigan
2	Keith Wood (captain) (Shane Byrne, 62)
1	Marcus Horan (John Hayes, 55)

Tries: Hickie 2, Horgan, Wood, Costello
Cons: Humphreys 3, O'Gara
Pens: Humphreys 4

ROMANIA
15	Danut Dumbrava (Ioan Teodorescu, 62)
14	Cristian Sauan (Mihai Vioreanu, 55)
13	Valentin Maftei
12	Romeo Gontineac (captain)
11	Gabriel Brezoianu
10	Ionut Tofan
9	Lucian Sirbu (Iulian Andrei, 65-67, 74)
8	Cristian Petre (Marius Niculai, 43)
7	Ovidiu Tonita (Marian Tudori, 69)
6	George Chiriac
5	Augustin Petrichei
4	Sorin Socol
3	Marcel Socaciu (Petrisor Toderasc, 43)
2	Razvan Mavrodin
1	Petru Balan (Cezar Popescu, 55)

Tries: Maftei, penalty try
Cons: Tofan, Andrei
Pen: Tofan

MATCH 4 POOL B

Oliver Magne of France (right) and Rupeni Caucau of Fiji are banished.

FRANCE 61 FIJI 18
Suncorp Stadium, October 11
Crowd: 46,795
Referee: Alain Rolland
Touch judges: Alan Lewis, Steve Walsh

FRANCE
15	Nicolas Brusque
14	Aurelien Rougerie (Pepito Elhorga, 56)
13	Tony Marsh
12	Yanick Jauzion (Gerald Merceron, 77)
11	Christophe Dominici
10	Frédéric Michalak (Gérald Merceron, 76)
9	Fabien Galthié (captain)
8	Imanol Harinordoquy
7	Olivier Magne (Christian Labit, 75)
6	Serge Betsen
5	Jérôme Thion
4	Fabien Pelous (Olivier Brouzet, 70)
3	Jean-Baptiste Poux
2	Raphael Ibanez
1	Jean-Jacques Crenca

Unused replacements
16	Yannick Bru
17	Olivier Milloud

Tries: Jauzion 3, Dominici 2, Harinordoquy, Ibanez
Cons: Michalak 4
Pens: Michalak 6
Yellow card: Magne (64)

FIJI
15	Norman Ligairi (Waisale Serevi, 59)
14	Vilimoni Delasau (Marika Vunibaka, 66)
13	Aisea Tuilevu
12	Seru Rabeni
11	Rupeni Caucaunibuca
10	Nicky Little
9	Moses Rauluni Sami Rabaka, 78)
8	Alifereti Doviverata (captain)
7	Kitione Salawa (Vula Maimuri, 57)
6	Sisa Koyamaibole
5	Api Naevo (Kele Leawere, 69)
4	Ifereimi Rawaqa
3	Joeli Veitayaki (Naca Seru, 66)
2	Greg Smith
1	Richard Nyholt

Unused replacements
17	Bill Gadolo

Tries: Naevo, Caucaunibuca
Con: Little
Pens: Little 2
Yellow card: Caucaunibuca (64)

MATCH 5 POOL C

Down and out: Uruguay try to regroup.

SOUTH AFRICA 72 URUGUAY 6
Subiaco Oval, October 11
Crowd: 16,936
Referee: Paddy O'Brien
Touch judges: Peter Marshall, Joel Jutge

SOUTH AFRICA
15	Werner Greeff
14	Ashwin Willemse
13	Jaque Fourie
12	De Wet Barry
11	Thinus Delport (Ricardo Loubscher, 64)
10	Louis Koen (Derick Hougaard, 60)
9	Joost van der Westhuizen (captain) (Neil de Kock, 60)
8	Juan Smith
7	Danie Rossouw (Hendro Scholtz, 72)
6	Joe van Niekerk
5	Victor Matfield (Selborne Boome, 64)
4	Bakkies Botha
3	Richard Bands (Faan Rautenbach, 56)
2	Danie Coetzee (John Smit, 56)
1	Lawrence Sephaka

Tries: Van der Westhuizen 3, Botha 2, van Niekerk, Delport, Fourie, Bands, Rossouw, Scholtz, Greeff
Cons: Koen 5, Hougaard

URUGUAY
15	Joaquin Pastore
14	Alfonso Cardoso (Juan Ramon Menchaca, 45)
13	Diego Aguirre (captain)
12	Martin Mendaro
11	Emiliano Ibarra
10	Sebastian Aguirre
9	Emiliano Caffera (Bernardo Amarillo, 59)
8	Rodrigo Capo
7	Marcelo Gutierrez (Nicolas Grille, 45)
6	Nicolas Brignoni (Hernan Ponte, 58)
5	Juan Alzueta
4	Juan Carlos Bado
3	Pablo Lemoine (Guillermo Storace, 73)
2	Diego Lamelas (Juan Andres Perez, 68)
1	Rodrigo Sanchez (Eduardo Berruti, 35-37,68)

Pens: D. Aguirre 2

MATCH 6 POOL D

Try time: Gareth Thomas (11) and teammates celebrate one of five for Wales.

WALES 41 CANADA 10
Telstra Dome, October 12
Crowd: 24,874
Referee: Chris White
Touch judges: Andre Watson, George Ayoub

WALES
15	Kevin Morgan
14	Mark Jones
13	Sonny Parker
12	Iestyn Harris
11	Gareth Thomas
10	Ceri Sweeney (Mark Taylor, 65)
9	Gareth Cooper (Dwayne Peel, 65)
8	Colin Charvis (captain)
7	Martyn Williams
6	Dafydd Jones
5	Gareth Llewellyn
4	Brent Cockbain (Robert Sidoli, 53)
3	Gethin Jenkins (Adam Jones, 59)
2	Robin McBryde (Huw Bennett, 59)
1	Duncan Jones (Gethin Jenkins, 78)

Unused replacements:
19	Jonathan Thomas
22	Rhys Williams

Tries: Parker, Cooper, M. Jones, Charvis, Thomas
Cons: Harris 5
Pens: Harris 2
Yellow card: Charvis (9), Parker (71)

CANADA
15	James Pritchard
14	Winston Stanley
13	Nikyta Witkowski
12	Marco Di Girolamo
11	David Lougheed
10	Bob Ross (Ryan Smith, 60)
9	Morgan Williams
8	Josh Jackson
7	Adam van Staveren
6	Al Charron (captain) (Jamie Cudmore, 59)
5	Mike James
4	Colin Yukes
3	Jon Thiel (Garth Cooke, 30-34)
2	Mark Lawson
1	Rod Snow (Kevin Tkachuk, 59)

Unused replacements:
16	Aaron Abrams
20	Ryan Banks
21	Ed Fairhurst

Try: Tkachuk
Con: Pritchard
DG: Ross

MATCH 7 POOL B

No way through for Hirotoki Onozawa of Japan.

SCOTLAND 32 JAPAN 11
Dairy Farmers Stadium, October 12
Crowd: 19,170
Referee: Stuart Dickinson
Touch judges: Alan Lewis, Alain Rolland

SCOTLAND
15	Ben Hinshelwood
14	Chris Paterson (Simon Danielli, 79)
13	Andy Craig
12	James McLaren
11	Kenny Logan
10	Gordon Ross (Gregor Townsend, 66)
9	Bryan Redpath (captain)
8	Simon Taylor
7	Jon Petrie (Martin Leslie, 57)
6	Jason White
5	Stuart Grimes
4	Scott Murray (Ross Beattie, 66)
3	Bruce Douglas (Gavin Kerr, 73)
2	Rob Russell
1	Tom Smith

Unused replacements
16	Gordon Bulloch
20	Mike Blair

Tries: Paterson 2, Grimes, Taylor, Danielli
Cons: Paterson, Townsend
Pen: Paterson

JAPAN
15	Tsutomu Matsuda (Toru Kurihara, 71)
14	Daisuke Ohata
13	Ruben Parkinson
12	Yukio Motoki
11	Hirotoki Onozawa
10	Keiji Hirose (Andrew Miller, 50)
9	Takashi Tsuji (Yuji Sonoda, 50)
8	Takeomi Ito
7	Takuro Miuchi (captain)
6	Naoya Okubo (Yasunori Watanabe, 67)
5	Adam Parker
4	Hajime Kiso
3	Masahiko Toyoyama
2	Masao Amino (Masaaki Sakata, 40)
1	Shin Hasegawa

Unused replacements
16	Masahito Yamamoto
18	Hiroyuki Tanuma

Try: Onozawa
Pens: Hirose 2

MATCH 8 POOL C

Ben Cohen scores one of his two tries in England's tally of 12.

ENGLAND 84 GEORGIA 6
Subiaco Oval, October 12
Crowd: 25,501
Referee: Pablo Deluca
Touch judges: Peter Marshall, Kelvin Deaker

ENGLAND
15	Josh Lewsey
14	Jason Robinson
13	Will Greenwood
12	Mike Tindall (Dan Luger, 36)
11	Ben Cohen
10	Jonny Wilkinson (Paul Grayson, 47)
9	Matt Dawson (Andy Gomarsall, 36)
8	Lawrence Dallaglio
7	Neil Back
6	Richard Hill (Lewis Moody, 50)
5	Ben Kay
4	Martin Johnson (captain)
3	Phil Vickery (Jason Leonard, 49)
2	Steve Thompson (Mark Regan, 40)
1	Trevor Woodman (Jason Leonard, 29-30)

Unused replacement
18	Danny Grewcock

Tries: Greenwood 2, Cohen 2, Tindall,
Dawson, Thompson, Back, Dallaglio, Regan,
Robinson, Luger
Cons: Wilkinson 5, Grayson 4
Pens: Wilkinson 2

GEORGIA
15	Besik Khamashuridze (Badri Khekhelashvili, 76)
14	Malkhaz Urjukashvili
13	Tedo Zibzibadze
12	Irakli Giorgadze
11	Vasil Katsadze (captain)
10	Paliko Jimsheladze (Merab Kvirikashvili, 76)
9	Irakli Abuseridze
8	George Chkhaidze (Irakli Machkhaneli, 79)
7	Gregoire Yachvili (David Bolgashvili, 67)
6	Gia Labadze
5	Victor Didebulidze (Vano Nadiradze, 44-46, 52)
4	Zurab Mchedlishvili
3	Aleko Margvelashvili (Soso Nikolaenko, 40)
2	Akvsenti Giorgadze (David Dadunashvili, 73)
1	Goderdzi Shvelidze

Pens: Urjukashvili, Jimsheladze

MATCH 9 POOL A

Gonzalo Quesada of Argentina had a good night in front of goal.

ARGENTINA 67 NAMIBIA 14
Central Coast Stadium, October 14
Crowd: 17,887
Referee: Nigel Williams
Touch judges: Paul Honiss, Alan Lewis

ARGENTINA
15	Juan Martin Hernandez
14	Hernan Senillosa
13	Martin Gaitan
12	Juan Fernandez Miranda (Felipe Contepomi, 41)
11	Diego Albanese
10	Gonzalo Quesada
9	Nicholas Fernandez Miranda (captain)
8	Pablo Bouza
7	Lucas Ostiglia
6	Martín Durand
5	Rimas Alvarez
4	Pedro Sporleder (Ignacio Fernandez Lobbe, 72)
3	Martin Scelzo (Rodrigo Roncero, 58)
2	Federico Mendez (Mario Ledesma, 46-49)
1	Mauricio Reggiardo

Unused replacements
18	Patricio Albacete
20	Agustin Pichot
22	Ignacio Corleto

Tries: Gaitan 3, Bouza 2, Mendez, J. Fernandez
Miranda, N. Fernandez Miranda, penalty tries 2
Cons: Quesada 7
Pen: Quesada

NAMIBIA
15	Jurie Booysen (Neil Swanepoel, 79)
14	Deon Mouton
13	Du Preez Grobler
12	Corné Powell
11	Melrick Africa (Vincent Dreyer, 12-23, 40)
10	Emile Wessels (Neil Swanepoel, 23-32)
9	Hakkies Hüsselman (Ronaldo Pedro, 72)
8	Sean Furter (captain)
7	Herman Lintvelt (Jurgens van Lill, 65)
6	Schalk van der Merwe
5	Eben Isaacs (Wolfie Duvenhage, 28)
4	Heino Senekal
3	Neil du Toit (Andries Blaauw, 63)
2	Johannes Meyer
1	Kees Lensing

Unused replacement
16	Cor van Tonder

Tries: Grobler, Husselman
Cons: Wessels 2

MATCH 10 POOL B

Ifereimi Rawaqa of Fiji.

FIJI 19 USA 18
Suncorp Stadium, October 15
Crowd: 30,990
Referee: Joel Jutge
Touch judges: Andrew Cole, Nigel Whitehouse

FIJI
15	Alfred Uluinayau
14	Marika Vunibaka
13	Aisea Tuilevu
12	Seru Rabeni
11	Vilimoni Delasau
10	Nicky Little
9	Moses Rauluni
8	Alifereti Doviverata (captain)
7	Koli Sewabu
6	Alivereti Mocelutu (Sisa Koyamaibole, 56)
5	Api Naevo (Vula Maimuri, 67)
4	Ifereimi Rawaqa
3	Nacanieli Seru (Richard Nyholt, 57)
2	Greg Smith
1	Joeli Veitayaki

Unused replacements
16	Bill Gadolo
20	Waisale Serevi
21	Epeli Ruivadra
22	Norman Ligairi

Try: Naevo
Con: Little
Pens: Little 4

USA
15	Paul Emerick (John Buchholz, 71)
14	David Fee (John Buchholz, 56-66)
13	Phillip Eloff (Kain Cross, 73-77)
12	Kain Cross (Salesi Sika, 72)
11	Riaan van Zyl
10	Mike Hercus
9	Kevin Dalzell
8	Dan Lyle
7	David Hodges (captain)
6	Kort Schubert
5	Luke Gross
4	Alec Parker
3	Dan Dorsey
2	Kirk Khasigian
1	Mike MacDonald

Unused replacements
16	Matt Wyatt
17	John Tarpoff
18	Gerhard Klerck
19	Jurie Gouws
20	Kimball Kjar

Tries: Van Zyl, Schubert
Con: Hercus
Pens: Hercus 2

MATCH 11 POOL D

Breathtaking: Tonga's Viliami Vaki is stopped in his tracks.

ITALY 36 TONGA 12
Canberra Stadium, October 15
Crowd: 18,967
Referee: Steve Walsh
Touch judges: Alain Rolland, Iain Ramage

ITALY
15	Gonzalo Canale
14	Nicola Mazzucato
13	Christian Stoica (Andrea Masi, 75)
12	Manuel Dallan
11	Denis Dallan
10	Rima Wakarua
9	Alessandro Troncon (captain)
8	Sergio Parisse
7	Aaron Persico
6	Andrea de Rossi (Carlo Festuccia, 71)
5	Marco Bortolami
4	Santiago Dellape (Carlo Checchinato, 67)
3	Martin Castrogiovanni (Salvatore Perugini, 74)
2	Fabio Ongaro (Mauro Bergamasco, 75)
1	Andrea Lo Cicero

Unused replacements
17	Salvatore Perugini
20	Matteo Mazzantini
21	Francesco Mazzariol

Tries: D. Dallan 2, M. Dallan,
Cons: Wakarua 3
Pens: Wakarua 5
Yellow card: Ongaro (69)

TONGA
15	Pierre Hola
14	Sione Fonua
13	Gus Leger (Johnny Ngauamo, 55)
12	John Payne (Johnny Ngauamo, 50-52)
11	Tevita Tu'ifua
10	Sateki Tu'ipulotu
9	Sililo Martens
8	Benhur Kivalu (Usaia Latu, 43-46, Sione Fonua, 79)
7	Ipolito Fenukitau (Stanley Afeaki, 13)
6	Inoke Afeaki (Usaia Latu, 56)
5	Viliami Vaki
4	Milton Ngauamo
3	Heamani Lavaka (Sila Va'enuku, 74)
2	Ephram Taukafa (Viliami Ma'asi, 69)
1	Tonga Lea'aetoa (Kisi Pulu, 73)

Unused replacements
20	Tony Alatini

Tries: Payne, Tu'ifua
Con: Tu'ipulotu
Yellow cards: Fenukitau (2), Vaki (67)

MATCH 12 POOL C

Hard day at the office for Uruguay's Nicolas Brignoni.

SAMOA 60 URUGUAY 13
Subiaco Oval, October 15
Crowd: 22,020
Referee: David McHugh
Touch judges: Jonathan Kaplan, Andy Turner

SAMOA
15	Tanner Vili
14	Lome Fa'atau
13	Terry Fanolua (Dale Rasmussen, 67)
12	Brian Lima
11	Sailosi Tagicakibau
10	Earl Va'a (Dominic Feaunati, 49)
9	Steven So'oialo (Denning Tyrell 76)
8	Semo Sititi (captain) (Des Tuiavi'i, 74)
7	Maurie Fa'asavalu
6	Peter Poulos
5	Leo Lafaiali'i (Kitiona Viliamu, 55)
4	Opeta Palepoi
3	Jeremy Tomuli
2	John Meredith (Mahonri Schwalger 60)
1	Kas Lealamanu'a (Simon Lemalu, 51)

Tries: Lima 2, Fa'asavalu 2, Fa'atau, Feaunati, Lemalu, Palepoi, Tagicakibau, Vili
Cons: Va'a 3, Lemalu, Vili
Yellow card: Fa'atau (74)

URUGUAY
15	Juan Menchaca
14	Joaquin Pastore (Jose Viana, 59)
13	Diego Aguirre (captain)
12	Martin Mendaro (Joaquin de Freitas, 40)
11	Carlos Baldasarri
10	Bernardo Amarillo
9	Juan Campomar
8	Rodrigo Capo
7	Nicolas Grille (Nicolas Brignoni, 56)
6	Marcelo Gutierrez (Ignacio Conti, 56)
5	Juan Alzueta (Juan Alvarez, 59)
4	Juan Carlos Bado
3	Pablo Lemoine
2	Diego Lamelas (Juan Andres Perez, 71)
1	Rodrigo Sanchez (Juan Machado, 9-10, 71)

Tries: Capo, Lemoine
Pen: Aguirre

MATCH 13 POOL D

Mils Muliaina of New Zealand scores one of his four tries as Canada's Matt King attempts a tackle.

NEW ZEALAND 68 CANADA 6
Telstra Dome, October 17
Crowd: 38,899
Referee: Tony Spreadbury
Touch judges: Stuart Dickinson, George Ayoub

NEW ZEALAND
15	Leon MacDonald (Doug Howlett, 67)
14	Mils Muliaina
13	Ma'a Nonu
12	Daniel Carter
11	Caleb Ralph
10	Carlos Spencer
9	Steve Devine
8	Rodney So'oialo (Richie McCaw, 66)
7	Marty Holah (Daniel Braid, 68)
6	Reuben Thorne (captain)
5	Chris Jack
4	Brad Thorn
3	Kees Meeuws
2	Mark Hammett (Corey Flynn, 71)
1	Carl Hoeft

Unused replacements
17	Dave Hewett
20	Byron Kelleher
22	Greg Somerville

Tries: Muliaina 4, Ralph 2, So'oialo 2, Meeuws, Nonu
Cons: Carter 9

CANADA
15	Quentin Fyffe
14	Matt King
13	John Cannon (Nikyta Witkowski, 68)
12	Marco di Girolamo
11	Sean Fauth
10	Jared Barker (Ryan Smith, 78)
9	Ed Fairhurst
8	Jeff Reid
7	Jim Douglas (Adam van Staveren, 53)
6	Ryan Banks (captain) (Colin Yukes, 47)
5	Ed Knaggs
4	Jamie Cudmore
3	Garth Cooke (Rod Snow, 53)
2	Aaron Abrams
1	Kevin Tkachuk

Unused replacements
16	Mark Lawson
20	Morgan Williams

Pens: Barker 2

MATCH 14 POOL A

Australia's Elton Flatley celebrates with teammates after scoring the fastest try in RWC history.

AUSTRALIA 90 ROMANIA 8
Suncorp Stadium, October 18
Crowd: 48,778
Referee: Pablo Deluca
Touch judges: Joel Jutge, Kelvin Deaker

AUSTRALIA
15	Mat Rogers
14	Wendell Sailor
13	Matt Burke (Stirling Mortlock, 45)
12	Elton Flatley
11	Joe Roff
10	Stephen Larkham
9	George Gregan (captain) (Matt Giteau, 41)
8	David Lyons (Matt Cockbain, 57)
7	Phil Waugh (Lote Tuqiri, 64)
6	George Smith
5	Nathan Sharpe
4	Daniel Vickerman (Justin Harrison, 52)
3	Al Baxter (Ben Darwin, 45)
2	Brendan Cannon (Jeremy Paul, 53)
1	Bill Young

Tries: Flatley, Rogers 3, Burke 2, Larkham 2, Mortlock, Roff, Giteau, Tuqiri, Smith
Cons: Flatley 11
Pen: Flatley

ROMANIA
15	Danut Dumbrava
14	Gabriel Brezoianu (Ioan Teodorescu, 52-56)
13	Valentin Maftei
12	Romeo Gontineac (captain)
11	Cristian Sauan (Ioan Teodorescu, 57)
10	Ionut Tofan (Mihai Vioreanu, 41)
9	Lucian Sirbu (Cristian Podea, 64)
8	George Chiriac
7	Ovidiu Tonita (Bogdan Tudor, 64)
6	Marius Niculai (Marian Tudori, 10)
5	Cristian Petre
4	Sorin Socol
3	Silviu Florea (Cezar Popescu, 50)
2	Razvan Mavrodin (Marcel Socaciu, 50)
1	Petrisor Toderasc

Try: Toderasc
Pen: Tofan
Yellow card: Maftei (58)

MATCH 15 POOL B

Jean-Jacques Crenca of France takes on the Japanese defence.

FRANCE 51 JAPAN 29
Dairy Farmers Stadium, October 18
Crowd: 21,309
Referee: Alan Lewis
Touch judges: Steve Walsh, Mark Lawrence

FRANCE
15	Clément Poitrenaud
14	Aurélien Rougerie
13	Tony Marsh
12	Damien Traille
11	Christophe Dominici
10	Frédéric Michalak (Gérald Merceron, 70)
9	Fabian Galthié (captain)
8	Christian Labit
7	Olivier Magne
6	Serge Betsen (Sebastien Chabal, 70)
5	Olivier Brouzet
4	Fabien Pelous (David Auradou, 63)
3	Jean-Baptiste Poux (Jean-Jaques Crenca, 51-57)
2	Yannick Bru (Raphael Ibanez, 52)
1	Olivier Milloud (Jean-Jaques Crenca, 57)

Unused replacements
21	Yannick Jauzion
22	Pepito Elhorga

Tries: Rougerie 2, Michalak, Pelous, Dominici, Crenca
Cons: Michalak 5, Merceron
Pens: Michalak 3

JAPAN
15	Toru Kurihara
14	Daisuke Ohata
13	George Konia
12	Hideki Namba
11	Hirotoki Onozawa
10	Andrew Miller
9	Yuji Sonoda
8	Takeomi Ito
7	Takuro Miuchi (captain)
6	Naoya Okubo (Ryota Asano, 69)
5	Adam Parker
4	Hiroyuki Tanuma (Koichi Kubo, 43)
3	Ryo Yamamura
2	Masaaki Sakata
1	Shin Hasegawa

Unused replacements
16	Masahito Yamamoto
17	Masao Amino
20	Takashi Tsuji
21	Yukio Motoki
22	Takashi Yoshida

Tries: Konia, Ohata
Cons: Kurihara 2
Pens: Kurihara 5

MATCH 16 POOL C

Will Greenwood for England scores the only try of the match against South Africa.

SOUTH AFRICA 6 ENGLAND 25
Subiaco Oval, October 18
Crowd: 38,834
Referee: Peter Marshall
Touch judges: David McHugh, Donal Courtney

SOUTH AFRICA
15	Jaco van der Westhuyzen
14	Ashwin Willemse
13	Jorrie Muller
12	De Wet Barry
11	Thinus Delport (Werner Greeff, 77-78)
10	Louis Koen (Derick Hougaard, 69)
9	Joost van der Westhuizen
8	Juan Smith
7	Joe van Niekerk
6	Corné Krige (captain)
5	Victor Matfield
4	Bakkies Botha
3	Richard Bands (Lawrence Sephaka, 7-14, 69)
2	Danie Coetzee (John Smit 45-52, 58)
1	Christo Bezuidenhout

Unused replacements
18	Selborne Boome
19	Danie Rossouw
20	Neil de Kock

Pens: Koen 2

ENGLAND
15	Josh Lewsey
14	Jason Robinson
13	Will Greenwood
12	Mike Tindall (Dan Luger, 71)
11	Ben Cohen
10	Jonny Wilkinson
9	Kyran Bracken
8	Lawrence Dallaglio
7	Neil Back (Joe Worsley, 47-52)
6	Lewis Moody
5	Ben Kay
4	Martin Johnson (captain)
3	Phil Vickery
2	Steve Thompson
1	Trevor Woodman (Jason Leonard, 74)

Unused replacements
16	Dorian West
18	Martin Corry
20	Andy Gomarsall
21	Paul Grayson

Try: Greenwood
Con: Wilkinson
Pens: Wilkinson 4
DGs: Wilkinson 2

MATCH 17 POOL D

Sililo Martens of Tonga charges through the Welsh defence.

WALES 27 TONGA 20
Canberra Stadium, October 19
Crowd: 19,806
Referee: Paul Honiss
Touch judges: Pablo Deluca, George Ayoub

WALES
15	Rhys Williams
14	Mark Jones
13	Mark Taylor
12	Iestyn Harris
11	Tom Shanklin
10	Stephen Jones
9	Gareth Cooper (Dwayne Peel, 56)
8	Alix Popham (Martyn Williams, 60)
7	Colin Charvis (captain)
6	Dafydd Jones
5	Robert Sidoli
4	Gareth Llewellyn (Chris Wyatt, 58)
3	Gethin Jenkins
2	Mefin Davies (Huw Bennett, 72)
1	Iestyn Thomas (Adam Jones, 63)

Unused replacements
21	Shane Williams
22	Garan Evans

Tries: Cooper, M. Williams
Con: S. Jones
Pens: S. Jones 4
DG: M. Williams

TONGA
15	Sila Va'enuku
14	Sione Fonua
13	Sukanaivalu Hufanga
12	John Payne
11	Tevita Tu'ifua
10	Pierre Hola
9	Sililo Martens
8	Benhur Kivalu (captain)
7	Stanley Afeaki (Milton Ngauamo, 64)
6	Ipolito Fenukitau (Nisifolo Naufahu, 73)
5	Viliami Vaki
4	Usaia Latu
3	Heamani Lavaka
2	Viliami Ma'asi (Ephram Taukafa, 71)
1	Kisi Pulu (Tonga Lea'aetoa, 72)

Unused replacements
20	David Palu
21	Sateka Tui'ipulotu
22	Gus Leger

Tries: Hola, Kivalu, Lavaka
Con: Hola
Pen: Hola

MATCH 18 POOL A

Flanker Paul O'Connell masterminds another Irish forward move.

IRELAND 64 NAMIBIA 7
Aussie Stadium, October 19
Crowd: 35,382
Referee: Andrew Cole
Touch judges: Stuart Dickinson, Joel Dume

IRELAND
15	Girvan Dempsey (John Kelly, 65)
14	Shane Horgan
13	Brian O'Driscoll
12	Kevin Maggs
11	Denis Hickie
10	Ronan O'Gara
9	Peter Stringer (Guy Easterby, 53)
8	Eric Miller
7	Alan Quinlan
6	Simon Easterby
5	Paul O'Connell
4	Malcolm O'Kelly
3	John Hayes (Simon Best, 72)
2	Keith Wood (captain) (Shane Byrne, 53)
1	Marcus Horan

Unused replacements
18	Donnacha O'Callaghan
19	Victor Costello
21	David Humphreys

Tries: Miller 2, Quinlan 2, Dempsey, Hickie, Horan, G. Easterby, Horgan, Kelly
Cons: O'Gara 7

NAMIBIA
15	Ronaldo Pedro
14	Deon Mouton
13	Du Preez Grobler
12	Corné Powell (Melrick Africa, 72)
11	Vincent Dreyer
10	Emile Wessels (Morné Schreuder, 62)
9	Hakkies Hüsselman (Neil Swanepoel, 62)
8	Sean Furter (captain) (Jurgens van Lill, 63)
7	Wolfie Duvenhage (Herman Lintvelt, 66)
6	Schalk van der Merwe
5	Archie Graham
4	Heino Senekal
3	Neil du Toit (Andries Blaauw, 60)
2	Johannes Meyer (Cor van Tonder, 26)
1	Kees Lensing

Try: Powell
Con: Wessels
Yellow card: Senekal (20)

MATCH 19 POOL C

Georgia's drop-kick expert Paliko Jimsheladze has another shot at goal.

GEORGIA 9 SAMOA 46
Subiaco Oval, October 19
Crowd: 21,507
Referee: Alain Rolland
Touch judges: David McHugh, Donal Courtney

GEORGIA
15	Badri Khekhelashvili (Besik Khamashuridze, 40)
14	Malkhaz Urjukashvili
13	Tedo Zibzibadze
12	Irakli Giorgadze
11	Vasil Katsadze (Irakli Machkhaneli, 40)
10	Paliko Jimsheladze
9	Irakli Abuseridze (Merab Kvirikashvili, 34)
8	Ilia Zedginidze (captain)
7	Gregoire Yachvili
6	Gia Labadze (David Bolgashvili, 63)
5	Vano Nadiradze (Victor Didebulidze, 57)
4	Zurab Mchedlishvili
3	Soso Nikolaenko (Aleko Margvelashvili, 68)
2	Akvsenti Giorgadze
1	Goderdzi Shvelidze

Unused replacements
16 David Dadunashvili

Pens: Jimsheladze 2
DG: Jimsheladze
Yellow card: Machkhaneli

SAMOA
15	Tanner Vili
14	Ron Fanuatanu (Dominic Feaunati, 7)
13	Terry Fanolua (Dale Rasmussen, 53)
12	Brian Lima
11	Sailosi Tagicakibau
10	Earl Va'a
9	Steven So'oialo (Denning Tyrell, 74)
8	Semo Sititi (captain)
7	Maurie Fa'asavalu (Siaosi Vaili, 53)
6	Peter Poulos
5	Leo Lafaiali'i
4	Opeta Palepoi (Kitiona Viliamu, 63)
3	Jeremy Tomuli
2	John Meredith (Mahonri Schwalger, 79)
1	Kas Lealamanu'a (Simon Lemalu, 68)

Tries: Feaunati, Lima, Sititi, So'oialo, Tagicakibau, Va'a
Cons: Va'a 5
Pens: Va'a 2

MATCH 20 POOL B

Gregor Townsend (centre) celebrates his try for Scotland.

SCOTLAND 39 USA 15
Suncorp Stadium, October 20
Crowd: 46,796
Referee: Jonathan Kaplan
Touch judges: Joel Jutge, Andy Turner

SCOTLAND
15	Glenn Metcalfe
14	Simon Danielli
13	Andy Craig (Ben Hinshelwood, 72)
12	Andrew Henderson
11	Chris Paterson
10	Gregor Townsend (Kenny Logan, 77)
9	Mike Blair (Bryan Redpath, 60)
8	Simon Taylor
7	Jon Petrie (Martin Leslie, 53)
6	Ross Beattie (Jason White, 66)
5	Stuart Grimes
4	Nathan Hines
3	Gavin Kerr
2	Gordon Bulloch (captain)
1	Tom Smith (Bruce Douglas, 43-51, 73)

Unused replacement
16 Rob Russell

Tries: Danielli 2, Kerr, Townsend, Paterson
Cons: Paterson 4
Pens: Paterson 2
Yellow card: Smith (40+)

USA
15	Paul Emerick
14	David Fee
13	Phillip Eloff
12	Kain Cross (Jason Keyter, 43)
11	Riaan van Zyl (Link Wilfley, 80)
10	Mike Hercus
9	Kevin Dalzell (Kimball Kjar, 66)
8	Dan Lyle
7	David Hodges (captain) (Jurie Gouws, 30-38), (Oloseti Fifita, 69)
6	Kort Schubert
5	Luke Gross
4	Alec Parker (Jurie Gouws, 53-60)
3	Dan Dorsey (Richard Liddington, 66)
2	Kirk Khasigian
1	Mike MacDonald

Unused replacement
16 Matt Wyatt

Pens: Hercus 5

MATCH 21 POOL D

Cristian Stoica of Italy is caught by a classic tackle.

ITALY 19 CANADA 14
Canberra Stadium, October 21
Crowd: 20,515
Referee: Paddy O'Brien
Touch judges: Pablo Deluca, Kelvin Deaker

ITALY
15	Gonzalo Canale
14	Mirco Bergamasco (Andrea Masi, 40, Francesco Mazzariol, 80)
13	Cristian Stoica
12	Manuel Dallan
11	Denis Dallan
10	Rima Wakarua
9	Alessandro Troncon (captain) (Matteo Mazzantini, 41)
8	Sergio Parisse
7	Aaron Persico (Scott Palmer, 56-65, 69, Carlo Festuccia, 79)
6	Andrea de Rossi (Aaron Persico, 73)
5	Marco Bortolami (Carlo Checchinato, 30)
4	Santiago Dellape
3	Martin Castrogiovanni
2	Fabio Ongaro
1	Andrea Lo Cicero

Unused replacement
17 Salvatore Perugini

Try: Parisse
Con: Wakarua
Pens: Wakarua 4
Yellow card: Ongaro (79)

CANADA
15	Quentin Fyffe
14	Winston Stanley
13	John Cannon
12	Marco di Girolamo
11	Dave Lougheed
10	Jared Barker
9	Morgan Williams
8	Ryan Banks (Josh Jackson, 32)
7	Jim Douglas
6	Jamie Cudmore
5	Al Charron (captain)
4	Colin Yukes
3	Jon Thiel (Rod Snow, 69)
2	Mark Lawson
1	Rod Snow (Kevin Tkachuk, 53)

Unused replacements
16	Aaron Abrams
18	Jeff Reid
20	Sean Fauth
21	Bob Ross
22	Matt King

Try: Fyffe
Pens: Barker 3
Yellow card: di Girolamo (51)

MATCH 22 POOL A

Juan Hernandez of Argentina touches down for one of his two tries against Romania.

ARGENTINA 50 ROMANIA 3
Aussie Stadium, October 22
Crowd: 33,673
Referee: Chris White
Touch judges: Steve Walsh, Nigel Whitehouse

ARGENTINA
15	Juan Martín Hernandez
14	Jose Maria Nunez Piossek (Agustin Pichot, 61)
13	Martin Gaitan
12	Manuel Contepomi
11	Hernan Senillosa
10	Juan Fernandez Miranda (Gonzalo Quesada, 61)
9	Nicolas Fernandez Miranda
8	Pablo Bouza
7	Martín Durand
6	Santiago Phelan (captain) (Rolando Martin, 20-22, 61)
5	Patricio Albacete
4	Pedro Sporleder
3	Martin Scelzo (Omar Hasan, 72)
2	Mario Ledesma
1	Rodrigo Roncero

Unused replacements
16	Federico Mendez
18	Rimas Alvarez
22	Jose Orengo

Tries: Hernandez 2, Gaitan, Contepomi, N. Fernandez Miranda, Bouza 2
Cons: J. Fernandez Miranda 4, Quesada 2
Pen: J. Fernandez Miranda

ROMANIA
15	Gabriel Brezoianu
14	Mihai Vioreanu (Vasile Ghioc, 75)
13	Valentin Maftei (Cristian Sauan, 56)
12	Romeo Gontineac (captain)
11	Ioan Teodorescu
10	Ionut Tofan
9	Lucian Sirbu (Iulian Andrei, 40)
8	George Chiriac (Agustin Petrichei, 40)
7	Ovidiu Tonita
6	Marian Tudori (Florin Tatu, 70)
5	Cristian Petre
4	Sorin Socol
3	Silviu Florea (Cezar Popescu, 40, Paulica Ion, 56)
2	Razvan Mavrodin
1	Petrisor Toderasc

Pen: Tofan

MATCH 23 POOL B

All of his team's points, all in vain: Andrew Miller of Japan shows his frustration.

FIJI 41 JAPAN 13
Dairy Farmers Stadium, October 23
Crowd: 17,269
Referee: Nigel Williams
Touch judges: Tony Spreadbury, Iain Ramage

FIJI
15	Norman Ligairi
14	Aisea Tuilevu
13	Epeli Ruivadra (Marika Vunibaka, 65)
12	Seru Rabeni
11	Vilimoni Delasau
10	Waisale Serevi (Nicky Little, 11)
9	Sami Rabaka (Moses Rauluni, 50)
8	Alifereti Doviverata (captain)
7	Koli Sewabu
6	Alivereti Mocelutu (Sisa Koyamaibole, 18)
5	Kele Leawere (Vula Maimuri, 57)
4	Emori Katalau
3	Nacanieli Seru (Joeli Veitayaki, 41)
2	Greg Smith (Bill Gadolo, 73)
1	Isaia Rasila

Tries: Ligairi 2, Tuilevu 2, Vunibaka
Cons: Little 2
Pens: Serevi 1, Little 3
Yellow card: Gadolo (79)

JAPAN
15	Tsutomu Matsuda (Toru Kurihara, 60)
14	Daisuke Ohata
13	Ruben Parkinson
12	Yukio Motoki
11	Hirotoki Onozawa (George Konia, 68)
10	Andrew Miller
9	Takashi Tsuji (Yuji Sonoda, 54)
8	Takeomi Ito (Ryota Asano, 72)
7	Takuro Miuchi
6	Naoya Okubo
5	Adam Parker (Masao Amino, 52)
4	Hajime Kiso (Koichi Kubo, 53-57)
3	Masahiko Toyoyama
2	Masaaki Sakata (Masao Amino, 54)
1	Masahito Yamamoto (Shin Hasegawa, 60)

Try: Miller
Con: Miller
Pen: Miller
DG: Miller

MATCH 24 POOL D

Daniel Carter of New Zealand takes on the Tonga defence.

NEW ZEALAND 91 TONGA 7
Suncorp Stadium, October 24
Crowd: 47,588
Referee: Pablo Deluca
Touch judges: Chris White, Donal Courtney

NEW ZEALAND
15	Mils Muliaina (Ben Atiga, 76)
14	Doug Howlett
13	Leon MacDonald
12	Daniel Carter
11	Caleb Ralph
10	Carlos Spencer
9	Justin Marshall (Ma'a Nonu, 76)
8	Rodney So'oialo
7	Daniel Braid (Marty Holah, 54)
6	Reuben Thorne (captain) (Richie McCaw, 61)
5	Ali Williams
4	Brad Thorn
3	Greg Somerville (Dave Hewett, 61)
2	Corey Flynn
1	Kees Meeuws

Unused replacements
16	Keven Mealamu
18	Jerry Collins

Tries: Braid, Carter, Flynn, Ralph 2, Spencer, Meeuws, Muliaina 2, MacDonald, Howlett 2, penalty try
Cons: MacDonald 12, Spencer

TONGA
15	Sila Va'enuku
14	Sione Fonua
13	Sukanaivalu Hufanga (Sateki Tu'ipulotu, 40)
12	John Payne
11	Tevita Tu'ifua (Gus Leger, 40)
10	Pierre Hola
9	Sililo Martens
8	Benhur Kivalu
7	Stanley Afeaki
6	Ipolito Fenukitau
5	Viliami Vaki (Edward Langi, 71)
4	Usaia Latu (Milton Ngauamo, 47)
3	Heamani Lavaka (Kisi Pulu, 74)
2	Viliami Ma'asi (Ephram Taukafa, 58)
1	Kisi Pulu (Tonga Lea'aetoa, 26)

Unused replacement
20	David Palu

Try: Hola
Con: Tu'ipulotu
Yellow card: Va'enuku (66)

MATCH 25 POOL C

South African flanker Danie Rossouw takes on the Georgian defence.

SOUTH AFRICA 46 GEORGIA 19
Aussie Stadium, October 24
Crowd: 34,308
Referee: Stuart Dickinson
Touch judges: Paul Honiss, Alan Lewis

SOUTH AFRICA

15	Ricardo Loubscher
14	Stefan Terblanche
13	Jaque Fourie
12	Werner Greeff (Jorrie Muller, 77)
11	Breyton Paulse
10	Derick Hougaard
9	Neil de Kock
8	Joe van Niekerk (Schalk Burger, 63)
7	Danie Rossouw
6	Hendro Scholtz
5	Selborne Boome
4	Bakkies Botha
3	Faan Rautenbach
2	John Smit (captain)
1	Lawrence Sephaka (Dale Santon, 68)

Unused replacements

17	Christo Bezuidenhout
18	Victor Matfield
20	Joost van der Westhuizen
21	Louis Koen

Tries: Rossouw 2, Hougaard, Van Niekerk, Fourie, Botha, Burger
Cons: Hougaard 4
Pen: Hougaard
Yellow card: Scholtz (53)

GEORGIA

15	Irakli Machkhaneli (Besik Khamashuridze, 61)
14	Gocha Khonelidze
13	Otar Eloshvili
12	Vasil Katsadze (captain)
11	Archil Kavtarashvili
10	Paliko Jimsheladze (Merab Kvirikashvili, 59)
9	Irakli Modebadze
8	George Chkhaidze (Ilia Zedginidze, 77)
7	David Bolgashvili (Irakli Abuseridze, 75)
6	George Tsiklauri
5	Victor Didebulidze
4	Sergo Gujaraidze
3	Alexandre Margvelashvili (Soso Nikolaenko, 75)
2	David Dadunashvili (Akvsenti Giorgadze, 75)
1	Avtandil Kopaliani

Unused replacement

19	Gregoire Yachvili

Try: Dadunashvili
Con: Jimsheladze
Pens: Jimsheladze 3, Kvirikashvili
Yellow card: Kvirikashvili

MATCH 26 POOL A

When you're down, you're down: a dejected Kees Lensing of Namibia.

AUSTRALIA 142 NAMIBIA 0
Adelaide Oval, October 25
Crowd: 28,196
Referee: Joel Jutge
Touch judges: Paddy O'Brien, Mark Lawrence

AUSTRALIA

15	Chris Latham
14	Lote Tuqiri
13	Stirling Mortlock (Matt Burke, 50)
12	Nathan Grey (Morgan Turinui, 50)
11	Mat Rogers
10	Matt Giteau
9	Chris Whitaker (captain)
8	David Lyons (John Roe, 40)
7	David Croft
6	George Smith (Matt Cockbain, 40)
5	Nathan Sharpe (David Giffin, 40)
4	Justin Harrison
3	Ben Darwin
2	Jeremy Paul
1	Matt Dunning

Unused replacements

16	Brendan Cannon
17	Bill Young

Tries: Latham 5, Tuqiri 3, Giteau 3, Rogers 2, Turinui 2, Lyons, Mortlock, Paul, Grey, Burke, Roe (penalty try)
Cons: Rogers 16

NAMIBIA

15	Ronaldo Pedro (Deon Grunschloss, 50-56, Sean Furter, 75)
14	Deon Mouton (Schalk van der Merwe, 29)
13	Du Preez Grobler (Phillipus Isaacs, 75)
12	Emile Wessels
11	Jurie Booysen (Melrick Africa, 12, Deon Grunschloss, 70)
10	Morné Schreuder
9	Hakkies Hüsselman (Neil Swanepoel, 49)
8	Jurgens van Lill
7	Herman Lintvelt
6	Shaun van Rooi
5	Eben Isaacs
4	Heino Senekal
3	Neil du Toit (Andries Blaauw, 55)
2	Cor van Tonder
1	Kees Lensing

MATCH 27 POOL D

Gareth Llewellyn of Wales catches the ball as Andrea Masi challenges.

ITALY 15 WALES 27
Canberra Stadium, October 25
Crowd: 22,641
Referee: Andrew Cole
Touch judges: Peter Marshall, Kelvin Deaker

ITALY

15	Gonzalo Canale (Francesco Mazzariol, 71)
14	Nicola Mazzucato
13	Cristian Stoica
12	Andrea Masi
11	Denis Dallan
10	Rima Wakarua
9	Alessandro Troncon (captain)
8	Sergio Parisse (Scott Palmer, 64)
7	Aaron Persico (Mauro Bergamasco, 44-51, Scott Palmer, 64)
6	Andrea de Rossi (Bergamasco, 57)
5	Santiago Dellape (Cristian Bezzi, 69)
4	Carlo Checchinato (Matthew Phillips, 50)
3	Martin Castrogiovanni
2	Fabio Ongaro (Carlo Festuccia, 47)
1	Andrea Lo Cicero (Salvatore Perugini, 68)

Pens: Wakarua 5

WALES

15	Kevin Morgan (Rhys Williams, 23)
14	Mark Jones
13	Sonny Parker (Dwayne Peel, 74)
12	Iestyn Harris
11	Gareth Thomas
10	Ceri Sweeney (Stephen Jones, 50)
9	Dwayne Peel (Gareth Cooper, 56)
8	Colin Charvis (captain)
7	Martyn Williams
6	Dafydd Jones
5	Gareth Llewellyn (Rob Sidoli, 50)
4	Brent Cockbain (Jonathan Thomas, 71)
3	Adam Jones
2	Robin McBryde
1	Duncan Jones (Gethin Jenkins, 25)

Unused replacement

16	Mefin Davies

Tries: M. Jones, Parker, D. Jones
Cons: Harris 3
Pen: Harris 2

MATCH 28 POOL B

Frédéric Michalak of France goes over for a try.

FRANCE 51 SCOTLAND 9
Telstra Stadium, October 25
Crowd: 78,974
Referee: David McHugh
Touch judges: Alain Rolland, Alan Lewis

FRANCE
15	Nicolas Brusque
14	Aurélien Rougerie
13	Tony Marsh (Damien Traille, 72)
12	Yannick Jauzion
11	Christophe Dominici
10	Frédéric Michalak
9	Fabien Galthié (captain) (Gérald Merceron, 76)
8	Imanol Harinordoquy (Olivier Brouzet, 78)
7	Olivier Magne (Patrick Tabacco, 66)
6	Serge Betsen
5	Jérôme Thion
4	Fabien Pelous
3	Sylvain Marconnet (Olivier Milloud, 65)
2	Raphael Ibanez (Yannick Bru, 65)
1	Jean-Jacques Crenca

Unused replacements
22	Pepito Elhorga

Tries: Betsen, Harinordoquy, Michalak, Galthié, Brusque
Cons: Michalak 4
Pens: Michalak 4
DGs: Michalak, Brusque

SCOTLAND
15	Glenn Metcalfe
14	Chris Paterson
13	Andy Craig
12	Andrew Henderson (James McLaren, 66)
11	Kenny Logan
10	Gregor Townsend
9	Bryan Redpath (captain)
8	Simon Taylor (Jon Petrie, 67)
7	Cameron Mather (Petrie, 36-40)
6	Jason White
5	Stuart Grimes
4	Scott Murray (Nathan Hines, 60)
3	Gavin Kerr (Bruce Douglas, 40)
2	Gordon Bulloch (Robbie Russell, 72)
1	Tom Smith

Unused replacements
20	Mike Blair
22	Simon Danielli

Pens: Paterson 3

MATCH 29 POOL A

Federico Mendez of Argentina shows the pain of his team's one-point loss.

ARGENTINA 15 IRELAND 16
Adelaide Oval, October 26
Crowd: 28,803
Referee: Andre Watson
Touch judges: Paddy O'Brien, Nigel Whitehouse

ARGENTINA
15	Ignacio Corleto
14	Jose Maria Nunez Piossek
13	Jose Orengo
12	Felipe Contepomi
11	Diego Albanese
10	Gonzalo Quesada
9	Agustin Pichot
8	Gonzalo Longo
7	Rolando Martin
6	Lucas Ostiglia
5	Rimas Álvarez
4	Ignacio Fernandez Lobbe
3	Mauricio Reggiardo (Martin Scelzo, 73)
2	Federico Mendez
1	Roberto Grau

Unused replacements
16	Mario Ledesma
18	Patricio Albacete
19	Santiago Phelan
20	Nicolas Fernandez Miranda
21	Martin Gaitan
22	Juan Martin Hernandez

Pens: Quesada 3
DGs: Quesada, Corleto

IRELAND
15	Girvan Dempsey
14	Shane Horgan
13	Brian O'Driscoll
12	Kevin Maggs
11	Denis Hickie
10	David Humphreys (Ronan O'Gara, 56)
9	Peter Stringer
8	Victor Costello
7	Alan Quinlan (Eric Miller, 20)
6	Simon Easterby
5	Paul O'Connell
4	Malcolm O'Kelly
3	John Hayes (Marcus Horan, 18-21)
2	Keith Wood (captain)
1	Reggie Corrigan (Marcus Horan, 56)

Unused replacements
16	Shane Byrne
18	Donnacha O'Callaghan
20	Guy Easterby
22	John Kelly

Try: Quinlan
Con: Humphreys
Pens: Humphreys, O'Gara 2

MATCH 30 POOL C

Iain Balshaw of England breaks the line.

ENGLAND 35 SAMOA 22
Telstra Dome, October 26
Crowd: 50,647
Referee: Jonathan Kaplan
Touch judges: Nigel Williams, Andy Turner

ENGLAND
15	Jason Robinson
14	Iain Balshaw
13	Stuart Abbott (Mike Catt, 71)
12	Mike Tindall
11	Ben Cohen
10	Jonny Wilkinson
9	Matt Dawson
8	Lawrence Dallaglio
7	Neil Back
6	Joe Worsley (Lewis Moody, 49)
5	Ben Kay
4	Martin Johnson (captain)
3	Julian White (Phil Vickery, 49)
2	Mark Regan (Steve Thompson, 49)
1	Jason Leonard

Unused replacements
18	Martin Corry
20	Andy Gomarsall
22	Dan Luger

Tries: Back, Balshaw, Vickery, penalty try
Cons: Wilkinson 3
Pens: Wilkinson 2
DG: Wilkinson

SAMOA
15	Tanner Vili
14	Lome Fa'atau
13	Terry Fanolua (Dale Rasmussen, 46)
12	Brian Lima
11	Sailosi Tagicakibau (Dominic Feaunati, 73)
10	Earl Va'a
9	Steven So'oialo (Denning Tyrell, 75)
8	Semo Sititi
7	Maurie Fa'asavalu
6	Peter Poulos (Kitiona Viliamu, 63)
5	Leo Lafaiali'i (Des Tuiavi'i, 66)
4	Opeta Palepoi
3	Jeremy Tomuli (Simon Lemalu, 53)
2	John Meredith (Mahonri Schwalger, 75)
1	Kas Lealamanu'a

Try: Sititi
Con: Va'a
Pens: Va'a 5

MATCH 31 POOL B

Kirk Khasigian of the USA in action during the match between Japan and USA.

JAPAN 26 USA 39
Central Coast Stadium, October 27
Crowd: 19,653
Referee: Steve Walsh
Touch judges: Alain Rolland, Iain Ramage

JAPAN
15	Tsutomu Matsuda (Hirotoki Onozawa, 40)
14	Daisuke Ohata
13	George Konia
12	Yukio Motoki
11	Toru Kurihara
10	Andrew Miller
9	Yuji Sonoda (Takashi Tsuji, 79)
8	Takeomi Ito (Yuya Saito, 56)
7	Takuro Miuchi (captain) (Yuya Saito, 24-28)
6	Naoya Okubo
5	Adam Parker
4	Hajime Kiso
3	Masahiko Toyoyama
2	Masao Amino
1	Shin Hasegawa (Masahito Yamamoto, 71)

Unused replacements
17	Masaaki Sakata
18	Koichi Kubo
21	Hideki Namba

Tries: Kurihara, Ohata
Cons: Kurihara 2
Pens: Kurihara 4

USA
15	Paul Emerick (John Buchholz, 44)
14	David Fee
13	Phillip Eloff
12	Salesi Sika
11	Riaan van Zyl
10	Mike Hercus
9	Kevin Dalzell (Kimball Kjar, 76-79)
8	Dan Lyle
7	David Hodges (captain)
6	Kort Schubert
5	Luke Gross
4	Gerhard Klerck
3	Dan Dorsey (Jacob Waasdorp, 79)
2	Kirk Khasigian (Matthew Wyatt, 14-17)
1	Mike MacDonald

Unused replacements
18	Jurie Gouws
19	Oloseti Fifita
21	Jason Keyter

Tries: Hercus, Eloff, Schubert, Van Zyl, Khasigian
Cons: Hercus 4
Pens: Hercus 2

MATCH 32 POOL C

Uruguayan players rush to congratulate Nicolas Brignoni after scoring a try.

GEORGIA 12 URUGUAY 24
Aussie Stadium, October 28
Crowd: 28,576
Referee: Kelvin Deaker
Touch judges: Nigel Williams, Donal Courtney

GEORGIA
15	Irakli Machkhaneli
14	Malkhaz Urjukashvili
13	Tedo Zibzibadze
12	Irakli Giorgadze (Vasil Katsadze, 59)
11	Archil Kavtarashvili (Besik Khamashuridze, 41)
10	Paliko Jimsheladze (Merab Kvirikashvili, 41)
9	Irakli Modebadze
8	Ilia Zedginidze
7	Gregoire Yachvili
6	George Chkhaidze
5	Sergo Gujaraidze (George Tsiklauri, 63)
4	Zurab Mchedlishvili
3	Avtandil Kopaliani (Soso Nikolaenko, 41-80)
2	David Dadunashvili (Akvsenti Giorgadze, 41)
1	Goderdzi Shvelidze

Unused replacement
19	David Bolgashvili

Pens: Urjukashvili, Kvirikashvili 3

URUGUAY
15	Juan Menchaca
14	Alfonso Cardoso
13	Diego Aguirre (captain)
12	Martin Mendaro (Joaquin Pastore, 50)
11	Carlos Baldasarri
10	Sebastian Aguirre
9	Juan Campomar (Bernardo Amarillo, 79)
8	Rodrigo Capo
7	Nicolas Grille
6	Hernan Ponte (Marcelo Gutierrez, 56)
5	Juan Alzueta (Nicolas Brignoni, 66)
4	Juan Carlos Bado
3	Pablo Lemoine (Guillermo Storace, 79)
2	Diego Lamelas (Juan Andres Perez, 70)
1	Rodrigo Sanchez (Eduardo Berruti, 74)

Tries: Cardoso, Lamelas, Brignoni
Cons: D. Aguirre 2, Menchaca
Pens: Menchaca

MATCH 33 POOL D

Al Charron in typically attacking mode in his last match for Canada, the victory over Tonga.

CANADA 24 TONGA 7
WIN Stadium, October 29
Crowd: 15,630
Referee: Alain Rolland
Touch judges: Chris White, Andy Turner

CANADA
15	Quentin Fyffe (James Pritchard, 75)
14	Sean Fauth
13	Nikyta Witkowski (Ryan Smith, 28-40)
12	Marco di Girolamo
11	Winston Stanley
10	Bob Ross
9	Morgan Williams (Ed Fairhurst, 76)
8	Josh Jackson
7	Adam van Staveren
6	Jamie Cudmore (Jeff Reid, 62)
5	Mike James (Colin Yukes, 69)
4	Al Charron (captain) (Aaron Abrams, 70)
3	Garth Cooke
2	Mark Lawson
1	Rod Snow (Kevin Tkachuk, 40)

Tries: Fauth, Abrams
Cons: Pritchard
Pens: Ross 4

TONGA
15	Gus Leger (David Palu, 68)
14	Pila Fifita
13	Johnny Ngauamo (Sukanaivalu Hufanga, 48)
12	John Payne
11	Sione Fonua (Viliami Vaki, 40)
10	Pierre Hola
9	Sililo Martens
8	Benhur Kivalu
7	Sione Tu'Amoheloa
6	Nisifolo Naufahu (Ipolito Fenukitau, 57)
5	Inoke Afeaki
4	Milton Ngauamo (Usaia Latu, 76)
3	Heamani Lavaka (Kafalosi Tonga, 56)
2	Ephram Taukafa (Viliami Ma'asi, 60)
1	Tonga Lea'aetoa

Try: I. Afeaki
Con: Hola
Yellow card: Palu (80)

MATCH 34 POOL A

Ronaldo Pedro of Namibia takes a knock.

NAMIBIA 7 ROMANIA 37
York Park, October 30
Crowd: 15,457
Referee: Peter Marshall
Touch judges: Joel Jutge, Mark Lawrence

NAMIBIA
15	Ronaldo Pedro
14	Deon Mouton
13	Du Preez Grobler
12	Emile Wessels
11	Rudi van Vuuren (Corné Powell, 35)
10	Morné Schreuder
9	Neil Swanepoel (Deon Grunschloss, 51) (Rudi van Vuuren, 71)
8	Sean Furter (Jurgens van Lill, 40)
7	Wolfie Duvenhage
6	Schalk van der Merwe
5	Eben Isaacs
4	Heino Senekal
3	Neil du Toit (Andries Blaauw, 40)
2	Johannes Meyer (Cor van Tonder, 28)
1	Kees Lensing

Unused Replacement:
18	Herman Lintvelt

Try: Isaacs
Con: Wessels

ROMANIA
15	Danut Dumbrava (Mihai Vioreanu, 51)
14	Ioan Teodorescu
13	Valentin Maftei (Cristian Sauan, 59)
12	Romeo Gontineac (captain)
11	Gabriel Brezoianu
10	Ionut Tofan
9	Lucian Sirbu (Iulian Andrei, 59)
8	Sorin Socol
7	Ovidiu Tonita
6	George Chiriac (Marian Tudori, 47)
5	Cristian Petre
4	Augustin Petrichei
3	Marcel Socaciu (Silviu Florea, 40)
2	Razvan Mavrodin (Cezar Popescu, 68)
1	Petru Balan (Petrisor Toderasc, 48)

Tries: Petrichei, Sirbu, Chiriac, Teodorescu, Sauan
Cons: Tofan 3
Pens: Tofan 2

MATCH 35 POOL B

Free-scoring French centre Brian Liebenberg drives forward.

FRANCE 41 USA 14
WIN Stadium, October 31
Crowd: 17,833
Referee: Paul Honiss
Touch judges: Andrew Cole, Kelvin Deaker

FRANCE
15	Clément Poitrenaud
14	Pepito Elhorga
13	Brian Liebenberg
12	Damien Traille
11	David Bory
10	Gérald Merceron
9	Dmitri Yachvili
8	Christian Labit
7	Patrick Tabacco
6	Sébastien Chabal
5	Olivier Brouzet
4	David Auradou
3	Jean-Baptiste Poux (Sylvain Marconnet, 40)
2	Yannick Bru (captain)
1	Olivier Milloud

Unused replacements
16	Raphael Ibanez
18	Jérôme Thion
19	Olivier Magne
20	Frédéric Michalak
21	Yannick Jauzion
22	Aurélien Rougerie

Tries: Liebenberg 3, Poux, Bru
Cons: Merceron 2
Pens: Merceron 3
DG: Yachvili
Yellow card: Chabal (76)

USA
15	John Buchholz (Matt Sherman, 44-45)
14	David Fee
13	Phillip Eloff
12	Salesi Sika (Jason Keyter, 68)
11	Riaan van Zyl
10	Mike Hercus (Matt Sherman, 75)
9	Kevin Dalzell (Mose Timoteo, 17-20, 30)
8	Dan Lyle (Jurie Gouws, 28)
7	Dave Hodges (captain)
6	Kort Schubert
5	Luke Gross
4	Alec Parker
3	Dan Dorsey (Jacob Waasdorp, 62)
2	Kirk Khasigian (Matt Wyatt, 72)
1	Mike MacDonald

Unused replacement:
18	Gerhard Klerck

Tries: Schubert, Hercus
Cons: Hercus 2

MATCH 36 POOL B

Gordon Bulloch and Bruce Douglas of Scotland celebrate their last-gasp victory.

SCOTLAND 22 FIJI 20
Aussie Stadium, November 1
Crowd: 38,137
Referee: Tony Spreadbury
Touch judges: Andre Watson, Mark Lawrence

SCOTLAND
15	Glenn Metcalfe (Ben Hinshelwood, 73)
14	Simon Danielli (James McLaren, 32-38, 41)
13	Gregor Townsend
12	Andrew Henderson
11	Kenny Logan
10	Chris Paterson
9	Bryan Redpath (captain)
8	Simon Taylor
7	Cameron Mather
6	Ross Beattie (Jason White, 45)
5	Stuart Grimes
4	Nathan Hines
3	Bruce Douglas
2	Gordon Bulloch (Rob Russell, 40-41)
1	Tom Smith

Unused replacements
17	Gordon McIlwham
19	Jon Petrie
20	Mike Blair

Try: Smith
Con: Paterson
Pens: Paterson 5

FIJI
15	Norman Ligairi
14	Aisea Tuilevu
13	Epeli Ruivadra (Vilimoni Delasau, 79)
12	Seru Rabeni (Isikeli Nacewa, 78)
11	Rupeni Caucaunibuca
10	Nicky Little
9	Moses Rauluni (Jacob Rauluni, 67)
8	Alifereti Doviverata
7	Koli Sewabu (Kitione Salawa, 69)
6	Vula Maimuri (Sisa Koyamaibole, 50)
5	Api Naevo
4	Ifereimi Rawaqa
3	Joeli Veitayaki
2	Greg Smith (Nacanieli Seru, 32)
1	Isaia Rasila

Unused replacements
17	Seta Tawake

Tries: Caucaunibuca 2
Cons: Little 2
Pens: Little 2
Yellow card: Naevo (76)

MATCH 37 POOL C

Derick Hougaard of South Africa drop kicks for goal.

SOUTH AFRICA 60 SAMOA 10
Suncorp Stadium, November 1
Crowd: 48,496
Referee: Chris White
Touch judges: Stuart Dickinson, Alan Lewis

SOUTH AFRICA
15	Jaco van der Westhuyzen
14	Ashwin Willemse
13	Jorrie Muller
12	De Wet Barry (Jaque Fourie, 70)
11	Thinus Delport
10	Derick Hougaard (Louis Koen, 68)
9	Joost van der Westhuizen (Neil de Kock, 72)
8	Juan Smith
7	Joe van Niekerk (Danie Rossouw, 40-41, 44)
6	Corné Krige (captain) (Schalk Burger, 68)
5	Victor Matfield
4	Bakkies Botha
3	Faan Rautenbach (Richard Bands, 56)
2	John Smit (Danie Coetzee, 56)
1	Christo Bezuidenhout (John Smit, 75)

Tries: Van Niekerk, Muller, Hougaard, Smith, Willemse, Fourie, Van der Westhuyzen, de Kock
Cons: Hougaard 5, Koen 2
Pen: Hougaard
DG: Hougaard

SAMOA
15	Tanner Vili
14	Lome Fa'atau
13	Romi Ropati (Dale Rasmussen, 63)
12	Brian Lima
11	Sailosi Tagicakibau
10	Earl Va'a (Dominic Feaunati, 59)
9	Steven So'oialo (Denning Tyrell, 73)
8	Semo Sititi (captain)
7	Maurie Fa'asavalu
6	Peter Poulos (Kitiona Viliamu, 51)
5	Leo Lafaiali'i
4	Opeta Palepoi (Des Tuiavi'i, 68)
3	Jeremy Tomuli (Tamato Leupolu, 40)
2	John Meredith
1	Kas Lealamanu'a

Unused replacements
16	Mahonri Schwalger

Try: Palepoi
Con: Va'a
Pen: Va'a

MATCH 38 POOL A

Australian captain George Gregan addresses his team after winning the match.

AUSTRALIA 17 IRELAND 16
Telstra Dome, November 1
Crowd: 54,206
Referee: Paddy O'Brien
Touch judges: Jonathan Kaplan, Iain Ramage

AUSTRALIA
15	Mat Rogers
14	Wendell Sailor
13	Matthew Burke (Lote Tuqiri, 64)
12	Elton Flatley
11	Joe Roff
10	Stephen Larkham (Matt Giteau, 68)
9	George Gregan (captain)
8	David Lyons (Matt Cockbain, 60)
7	Phil Waugh
6	George Smith
5	Nathan Sharpe
4	David Giffin (Daniel Vickerman, 64)
3	Ben Darwin (Al Baxter, 51)
2	Brendan Cannon (Jeremy Paul, 73)
1	Bill Young

Unused replacement
20	Chris Whitaker

Try: Smith
Pens: Flatley 3
DG: Gregan
Yellow card: Rogers (40)

IRELAND
15	Girvan Dempsey
14	Shane Horgan
13	Brian O'Driscoll
12	Kevin Maggs (Eric Miller, 57-62)
11	Simon Best (John Kelly, 40)
10	Ronan O'Gara (David Humphreys, 70)
9	Peter Stringer
8	Anthony Foley (Eric Miller, 73)
7	Keith Gleeson
6	Simon Easterby
5	Paul O'Connell (Donnacha O'Callaghan, 75)
4	Malcolm O'Kelly (Donnacha O'Callaghan, 54-60)
3	John Hayes
2	Keith Wood (captain)
1	Reggie Corrigan (Marcus Horan, 68)

Unused replacement
16	Shane Byrne
20	Guy Easterby

Try: O'Driscoll
Con: O'Gara
Pens: O'Gara 2
DG: O'Driscoll

MATCH 39 POOL C

England fullback Josh Lewsey races away to score his fifth try.

ENGLAND 111 URUGUAY 13
Suncorp Stadium, November 2
Crowd: 46,233
Referee: Nigel Williams
Touch judges: Stuart Dickinson, Nigel Whitehouse

ENGLAND
15	Josh Lewsey
14	Iain Balshaw (Jason Robinson, 44)
13	Stuart Abbott
12	Mike Catt
11	Dan Luger
10	Paul Grayson (Will Greenwood, 62)
9	Andy Gomarsall (Kyran Bracken, 62)
8	Lawrence Dallaglio
7	Lewis Moody
6	Joe Worsley
5	Danny Grewcock
4	Martin Corry (Martin Johnson, 44)
3	Phil Vickery (captain) (Julian White, 53)
2	Dorian West
1	Jason Leonard

Unused replacements
16	Steve Thompson
19	Ben Kay

Tries: Lewsey 5, Balshaw 2, Gomarsall 2, Catt 2, Robinson 2, Greenwood, Moody, Luger, Abbott
Cons: Grayson 11, Catt 2

URUGUAY
15	Juan Menchaca (Emiliano Caffera, 72)
14	Joaquin Pastore
13	Diego Aguirre (captain)
12	Joaquin de Freitas (Diego Reyes, 5-9, 35-40)
11	Jose Viana (Diego Reyes, 53)
10	Sebastian Aguirre
9	Juan Campomar
8	Rodrigo Capo
7	Nicolas Grille (Marcelo Gutierrez, 44)
6	Nicolas Brignoni
5	Juan Miguel Alvarez (Juan Alzueta, 53)
4	Juan Carlos Bado
3	Pablo Lemoine (Guillermo Storace, 70)
2	Diego Lamelas (Juan Andres Perez, 57)
1	Eduardo Berruti (Rodrigo Sanchez, 44)

Try: Lemoine
Con: Menchaca
Pen: Menchaca 2

MATCH 40 POOL D

Garan Evans of Wales is taken from the field on the medi-cab after an injury.

NEW ZEALAND 53 WALES 37
Telstra Stadium, November 2
Crowd: 80,012
Referee: Andre Watson
Touch judges: Peter Marshall, Alan Lewis

NEW ZEALAND

15	Mils Muliaina
14	Doug Howlett
13	Leon MacDonald
12	Aaron Mauger
11	Joe Rokocoko
10	Carlos Spencer
9	Justin Marshall
8	Jerry Collins (Rodney So'oialo, 33-36, Marty Holah, 52)
7	Richie McCaw
6	Reuben Thorne (captain)
5	Ali Williams
4	Brad Thorn
3	Greg Somerville
2	Keven Mealamu (Mark Hammett, 70)
1	Dave Hewett (Kees Meeuws, 50)

Unused replacements

20	Byron Kelleher
21	Daniel Carter
22	Ma'a Nonu

Tries: Rokocoko 2, Howlett 2, MacDonald, Williams, Spencer, Mauger
Cons: MacDonald 5
Pen: MacDonald

WALES

15	Garan Evans (Gareth Thomas, 5)
14	Shane Williams
13	Mark Taylor (Ceri Sweeney, 26-33)
12	Sonny Parker (Ceri Sweeney, 35)
11	Tom Shanklin
10	Stephen Jones
9	Gareth Cooper (Dwayne Peel, 76)
8	Alix Popham (Dafydd Jones, 64)
7	Colin Charvis (captain)
6	Jonathan Thomas
5	Rob Sidoli
4	Brent Cockbain (Chris Wyatt, 60)
3	Adam Jones (Gethin Jenkins, 33)
2	Robin McBryde (Mefin Davies, 62)
1	Iestyn Thomas

Tries: Taylor, Parker, Charvis, S. Williams
Cons: S. Jones 4
Pens: S. Jones 3

MATCH 41 QF1

Carlos Spencer of New Zealand makes another break.

NEW ZEALAND 29 SOUTH AFRICA 9
Telstra Dome, November 8
Crowd: 40,734
Referee: Tony Spreadbury
Touch judges: Peter Marshall, Andrew Cole

NEW ZEALAND

15	Mils Muliaina
14	Doug Howlett
13	Leon MacDonald
12	Aaron Mauger (Daniel Carter, 77)
11	Joe Rokocoko (Caleb Ralph, 78)
10	Carlos Spencer
9	Justin Marshall (Steve Devine, 77)
8	Jerry Collins
7	Richie McCaw (Marty Holah, 60-64, 74)
6	Reuben Thorne (captain)
5	Ali Williams
4	Chris Jack (Brad Thorn, 74)
3	Greg Somerville
2	Keven Mealamu (Mark Hammett, 74)
1	Dave Hewett (Kees Meeuws, 50)

Tries: MacDonald, Mealamu, Rokocoko
Con: MacDonald
Pens: MacDonald 3
DG: Mauger

SOUTH AFRICA

15	Jaco van der Westhuyzen
14	Ashwin Willemse
13	Jorrie Muller
12	De Wet Barry
11	Thinus Delport (Jaque Fourie, 40)
10	Derick Hougaard (Louis Koen, 74)
9	Joost van der Westhuizen (Neil de Kock, 77)
8	Juan Smith
7	Danie Rossouw (Schalk Burger, 62)
6	Corné Krige (captain)
5	Victor Matfield (Selborne Boome, 77)
4	Bakkies Botha
3	Faan Rautenbach (Richard Bands, 60)
2	John Smit (Danie Coetzee, 74)
1	Christo Bezuidenhout

Pens: Hougaard 3

MATCH 42 QF2

Australian winger Lote Tuqiri is tackled by Scotland fly-half Chris Paterson.

AUSTRALIA 33 SCOTLAND 16
Suncorp Stadium, November 8
Crowd: 45,412
Referee: Steve Walsh
Touch judges: Paddy O'Brien, Andre Watson

AUSTRALIA

15	Mat Rogers (Joe Roff, 60)
14	Wendell Sailor
13	Stirling Mortlock
12	Elton Flatley
11	Lote Tuqiri
10	Stephen Larkham (Matt Giteau, 54) (Daniel Vickerman, 74)
9	George Gregan (captain) (Chris Whitaker, 66)
8	David Lyons
7	Phil Waugh (Brendan Cannon, 76-77)
6	George Smith (Matt Cockbain, 40)
5	Nathan Sharpe
4	Justin Harrison
3	Ben Darwin (Al Baxter, 65)
2	Brendan Cannon (Jeremy Paul, 62)
1	Bill Young

Tries: Mortlock, Gregan, Lyons
Cons: Flatley 3
Pens: Flatley 4

SCOTLAND

15	Glenn Metcalfe (Ben Hinshelwood, 47)
14	Simon Danielli
13	Gregor Townsend (James McLaren, 76)
12	Andrew Henderson
11	Kenny Logan
10	Chris Paterson
9	Bryan Redpath (captain)
8	Simon Taylor
7	Cameron Mather
6	Jason White (Jon Petrie, 65)
5	Stuart Grimes (Scott Murray, 62)
4	Nathan Hines
3	Bruce Douglas (Gordon McIlwham, 69)
2	Gordon Bulloch (Rob Russell, 73)
1	Tom Smith

Unused replacement:

20	Michael Blair

Try: Russell
Con: Paterson
Pens: Paterson 2
DG: Paterson

MATCH 43 QF3

Imanol Harinordoquy scores France's third try.

FRANCE 43 IRELAND 21
Telstra Dome, November 9
Crowd: 33,134
Referee: Jonathan Kaplan
Touch judges: Chris White, Nigel Williams

FRANCE
15	Nicolas Brusque
14	Aurélien Rougerie
13	Tony Marsh
12	Yannick Jauzion (Brian Liebenberg, 52)
11	Christophe Dominici
10	Frédéric Michalak
9	Fabien Galthié (captain)
8	Imanol Harinordoquy (Patrick Tabacco, 75)
7	Olivier Magne (Yannick Bru, 65-75)
6	Serge Betsen
5	Jérôme Thion (Olivier Brouzet, 65) (Pepito Elhorga, 78)
4	Fabien Pelous
3	Sylvain Marconnet
2	Raphael Ibanez (Olivier Magne, 75)
1	Jean-Jacques Crenca (Olivier Milloud, 70)

Unused replacement:
20	Gérald Merceron

Tries: Magne, Dominici, Harinordoquy, Crenca
Cons: Michalak 4
Pens: Michalak 5
Yellow card: Ibanez (65)

IRELAND
15	Girvan Dempsey
14	Shane Horgan
13	Brian O'Driscoll
12	Kevin Maggs
11	John Kelly
10	Ronan O'Gara (David Humphreys, 48)
9	Peter Stringer (Guy Easterby, 72)
8	Victor Costello (Eric Miller, 65)
7	Keith Gleeson
6	Simon Easterby
5	Paul O'Connell
4	Malcolm O'Kelly
3	John Hayes
2	Keith Wood (captain)
1	Reggie Corrigan (Marcus Horan, 52)

Unused replacements:
16	Shane Byrne
18	Donnacha O'Callaghan
22	Anthony Horgan

Tries: Maggs, O'Driscoll 2
Cons: Humphreys 3

MATCH 44 QF4

Jason Robinson moves away to set up a try for England.

ENGLAND 28 WALES 17
Suncorp Stadium, November 9
Crowd: 45,252
Referee: Alain Rolland
Touch judges: David McHugh, Joel Jutge

ENGLAND
15	Jason Robinson
14	Dan Luger (Mike Catt, 40)
13	Will Greenwood (Stuart Abbott, 53)
12	Mike Tindall
11	Ben Cohen
10	Jonny Wilkinson
9	Matt Dawson (Kyran Bracken, 68)
8	Lawrence Dallaglio
7	Neil Back
6	Lewis Moody
5	Ben Kay
4	Martin Johnson (captain)
3	Phil Vickery
2	Steve Thompson
1	Jason Leonard (Trevor Woodman, 45)

Unused replacements:
16	Dorian West
18	Simon Shaw
19	Joe Worsley

Try: Greenwood
Con: Wilkinson
Pens: Wilkinson 6
DG: Wilkinson

WALES
15	Gareth Thomas
14	Mark Jones
13	Mark Taylor
12	Iestyn Harris
11	Shane Williams
10	Stephen Jones (Ceri Sweeney, 59-72)
9	Gareth Cooper (Dwayne Peel, 65)
8	Jonathan Thomas (Martyn Williams, 58)
7	Colin Charvis (captain)
6	Dafydd Jones
5	Robert Sidoli
4	Brent Cockbain (Gareth Llewellyn, 48)
3	Adam Jones (Gethin Jenkins, 29)
2	Robin McBryde (Mefin Davies, 64)
1	Iestyn Thomas

Unused replacement:
22	Kevin Morgan

Tries: S. Jones, Charvis, M. Williams
Con: Harris

MATCH 45 SF1

Stirling Mortlock breaks free of the New Zealand defence to score Australia's only try.

NEW ZEALAND 10 AUSTRALIA 22
Telstra Stadium, November 15
Crowd: 82,444
Referee: Chris White
Touch judges: Andre Watson, Joel Jutge

NEW ZEALAND
15	Mils Muliaina
14	Doug Howlett
13	Leon MacDonald
12	Aaron Mauger
11	Joe Rokocoko
10	Carlos Spencer
9	Justin Marshall (Byron Kelleher, 48)
8	Jerry Collins (Marty Holah, 73)
7	Richie McCaw
6	Reuben Thorne (captain)
5	Ali Williams (Brad Thorn, 58)
4	Chris Jack
3	Greg Somerville
2	Keven Mealamu
1	Dave Hewett (Kees Meeuws, 48-70)

Unused replacements:
16	Mark Hammett
21	Daniel Carter
22	Caleb Ralph

Try: Thorne
Con: MacDonald
Pen: MacDonald

AUSTRALIA
15	Mat Rogers (Joe Roff, 29-35)
14	Wendell Sailor
13	Stirling Mortlock (Joe Roff, 72)
12	Elton Flatley (Nathan Grey, 64-67)
11	Lote Tuqiri
10	Stephen Larkham
9	George Gregan (captain)
8	David Lyons
7	Phil Waugh
6	George Smith (Matt Cockbain, 72)
5	Nathan Sharpe (David Giffin 24-31, 40)
4	Justin Harrison
3	Ben Darwin (Al Baxter 49)
2	Brendan Cannon (Jeremy Paul, 49)
1	Bill Young

Unused replacement:
20	Chris Whitaker

Try: Mortlock
Con: Flatley
Pens: Flatley 5

MATCH 46 SF2

France's Imanol Harinordoquy stops England winger Jason Robinson in his tracks.

FRANCE 7 ENGLAND 24
Telstra Stadium, November 16
Crowd: 82,346
Referee: Paddy O'Brien
Touch judges: Stuart Dickinson, Nigel Williams

FRANCE
15	Nicolas Brusque
14	Aurélien Rougerie
13	Tony Marsh
12	Yannick Jauzion
11	Christophe Dominici
	(Clément Poitrenaud, 34)
10	Frédéric Michalak (Gérald Merceron, 64)
9	Fabien Galthié (captain)
8	Imanol Harinordoquy
7	Olivier Magne
6	Serge Betsen (Christian Labit, 64)
5	Jérôme Thion
4	Fabien Pelous
3	Sylvain Marconnet
2	Raphael Ibanez
1	Jean-Jacques Crenca (Olivier Milloud, 62)

Unused replacements:
16	Yannick Bru
18	David Auradou
21	Damien Traille

Try: Betsen
Con: Michalak
Yellow cards: Dominici (23), Betsen (53)

ENGLAND
15	Josh Lewsey
14	Jason Robinson
13	Will Greenwood
12	Mike Catt (Mike Tindall, 69)
11	Ben Cohen
10	Jonny Wilkinson
9	Matt Dawson (Kyran Bracken 40-41, 70)
8	Lawrence Dallaglio
7	Neil Back
6	Richard Hill (Lewis Moody, 73)
5	Ben Kay
4	Martin Johnson (captain)
3	Phil Vickery
	(Jason Leonard 4-5)
2	Steve Thompson (Dorian West, 79)
1	Trevor Woodman (Jason Leonard, 79)

Unused replacement:
18	Martin Corry
22	Iain Balshaw

Pens: Wilkinson 5
DGs: Wilkinson 3

MATCH 47 PLAYOFF

No escape for Frédéric Michalak of France.

NEW ZEALAND 40 FRANCE 13
Telstra Stadium, November 20
Crowd: 62,712
Referee: Chris White
Touch judges: Peter Marshall, David McHugh

NEW ZEALAND
15	Mils Muliaina
14	Doug Howlett
13	Leon MacDonald
	(Daniel Carter, 18; Caleb Ralph, 76)
12	Aaron Mauger (Daniel Carter, 77)
11	Joe Rokocoko
10	Carlos Spencer
9	Steve Devine
8	Jerry Collins (Marty Holah, 43)
7	Richie McCaw (Marty Holah, 15-21)
6	Reuben Thorne (captain)
5	Ali Williams (Brad Thorn, 48)
4	Chris Jack
3	Greg Somerville
2	Keven Mealamu (Mark Hammett, 71)
1	Dave Hewett (Carl Hoeft, 69)

Unused replacement:
20	Byron Kelleher

Tries: Jack, Howlett, Rokocoko, Thorn, Muliaina, Holah
Cons: MacDonald, Carter 4

FRANCE
15	Clément Poitrenaud (Nicolas Brusque, 27)
14	Pepito Elhorga
13	Tony Marsh (Brian Liebenberg, 40)
12	Damien Traille
11	David Bory
10	Gérald Merceron (Frédéric Michalak, 65)
9	Dmitri Yachvili
8	Christian Labit
7	Patrick Tabacco (Olivier Magne, 57)
6	Sébastien Chabal
5	Thibault Privat (Fabien Pelous, 40)
4	David Auradou
3	Jean-Baptiste Poux
	(Jean-Jacques Crenca, 40)
2	Yannick Bru (captain)
	(Raphael Ibanez, 54)
1	Sylvain Marconnet
	(Jean-Baptiste Poux, 59)

Try: Elhorga
Con: Yachvili
Pen: Yachvili
DG: Yachvili

MATCH 48 FINAL

The Rugby World Cup-winning moment: Jonny Wilkinson celebrates his drop goal.

AUSTRALIA 17 ENGLAND 20
Telstra Stadium, November 22
Crowd: 82,957
Referee: Andre Watson
Touch Judges: Paddy O'Brien, Paul Honiss

AUSTRALIA
15	Mat Rogers
14	Wendell Sailor (Joe Roff, 71)
13	Stirling Mortlock
12	Elton Flatley
11	Lote Tuqiri
10	Stephen Larkham
	(Matt Giteau, 19-31, 56-64, 6-14 et)
9	George Gregan (captain)
8	David Lyons (Matt Cockbain, 57)
7	Phil Waugh
6	George Smith
5	Nathan Sharpe (David Giffin, 48)
4	Justin Harrison
3	Al Baxter
2	Brendan Cannon (Jeremy Paul, 57)
1	Bill Young (Matt Dunning, 13 et)

Unused replacement:
20	Chris Whitaker

Try: Tuqiri
Pens: Flatley 4

ENGLAND
15	Josh Lewsey (Iain Balshaw, 6 et)
14	Jason Robinson
13	Will Greenwood
12	Mike Tindall (Mike Catt, 79)
11	Ben Cohen
10	Jonny Wilkinson
9	Matt Dawson
8	Lawrence Dallaglio
7	Neil Back
6	Richard Hill (Lewis Moody, 14 et)
5	Ben Kay
4	Martin Johnson (captain)
3	Phil Vickery (Jason Leonard, 1 et)
2	Steve Thompson
1	Trevor Woodman

Unused replacements:
16	Dorian West
18	Martin Corry
20	Kyran Bracken

Try: Robinson
Pens: Wilkinson 4
DG: Wilkinson

STATISTICAL REVIEW

Team-by-team

ARGENTINA
Matches: 4
Won: 2
Lost: 2
Pool result: 3rd, 11 points
Points for: 140
Points against: 57
Tries: 18
Bouza 4, Gaitan 4, Hernandez 2, N.F. Miranda 2, Corleto, Mendez, J.F. Miranda, M. Contepomi, penalty tries 2
Conversions: 13
Quesada 9, J.F. Miranda 4
Penalties: 6
Quesada 4, J.F. Miranda, F. Contepomi
Drop goals: 2
Quesada, Corleto
Leading point scorers:
33 Quesada
20 Bouza
20 Gaitan

AUSTRALIA
Matches: 7
Won: 6
Lost: 1
Pool result: 1st, 18 points
Rugby World Cup runner-up
Points for: 345
Points against: 78
Tries: 43
Rogers 5, Tuqiri 5, Latham 5, Giteau 4, Mortlock 4, Burke 3, Larkham 2, Smith 2, Turinui 2, Lyons 2, Roff 2, Sailor, Flatley, Paul, Grey, Roe, Gregan, penalty try
Conversions: 32
Flatley 16, Rogers 16
Penalties: 21
Flatley 21
Drop goals: 1
Gregan
Leading point scorers:
100 Flatley
57 Rogers
25 Tuqiri
25 Latham

CANADA
Matches: 4
Won: 1
Lost: 3
Pool result: 4th, 5 points
Points for: 54
Points against: 135
Tries: 4
Tkachuk, Fyffe, Fauth, Abrams
Conversions: 2
Pritchard 2
Penalties: 9
Barker 5, Ross 4
Drop goals: 1
Ross
Leading point scorers:
15 Barker, Ross
5 Tkachuk, Fyffe, Fauth, Abraams

ENGLAND
Matches: 7
Won: 7
Lost: 0
Pool result: 1st, 19 points
Rugby World Cup winner
Points for: 327
Points against: 88
Tries: 36
Greenwood 5, Lewsey 5, Robinson 4, Balshaw 3, Cohen 2, Back 2, Luger 2, Catt 2, Gomarsall 2, Dallaglio, Tindall, Dawson, Regan, Thompson, Vickery, Moody, Abbott, penalty try
Conversions: 27
Grayson 15, Wilkinson 10, Catt 2
Penalties: 23
Wilkinson 23
Drop goals: 8
Wilkinson 8
Leading point scorers:
113 Wilkinson
30 Grayson
25 Greenwood
25 Lewsey

FIJI
Matches: 4
Won: 2
Lost: 2
Pool result: 3rd 10 points
Points for: 98
Points against: 114
Tries: 10
Caucaunibuca 3, Naevo 2, Ligairi 2, Tuilevu 2, Vunibaka
Conversions: 6
Little 6
Penalties: 12
Little 11, Serevi
Leading point scorers:
45 Little
15 Caucaunibuca
10 Naevo, Ligairi, Tuilevu

NAMIBIA
Matches: 4
Won: 0
Lost: 4
Pool result: 5th 0 points
Points for: 28
Points against: 310
Tries: 4
Grobler, Husselman, Powell, Isaacs
Conversions: 4
Wessels 4
Leading point scorers:
8 Wessels

NEW ZEALAND
Matches: 7
Won: 6
Lost: 1
Pool result: 1st, 20 points
Eliminated in semi-final (Australia); beat France in playoff to finish third
Points for: 361
Points against: 101
Tries: 52
Howlett 7, Muliaina 7, Rokocoko 6, Spencer 4, MacDonald 4, Ralph 4, Thorn 2, Thorne 2, Carter 2, So'oialo 2, Meeuws 2, Marshall, Nonu, Braid, Flynn, Williams, Mauger, Mealamu, Jack, Holah, penalty try
Conversions: 40
MacDonald 20, Carter 19, Spencer
Penalties: 6
MacDonald 5, Spencer
Drop goals: 18
Mauger 18
Leading point scorers:
75 MacDonald
48 Carter
35 Howlett
35 Muliaina
30 Rokocoko

ROMANIA
Matches: 4
Won: 1
Lost: 3
Pool result: 4th, 5 points
Points for: 65
Points against: 192
Tries: 8
Maftei, Toderasc, Petrichei, Sirbu, Chiriac, Teodorescu, Sauan, penalty try
Conversions: 5
Tofan 4, Andrei
Penalties: 5
Tofan 5
Leading point scorers:
23 Tofan

SAMOA
Matches: 4
Won: 2
Lost: 2
Pool result: 3rd 10 points
Points for: 138
Points against: 117
Tries: 18
Lima 3, Fa'asavalu 2, Sititi 2, Palepoi 2, Feaunati 2, Tagicakibau 2, Fa'atau, Lemalu, Vili, So'oialo, Va'a
Conversions: 12
Va'a 10, Vili, Lemalu
Penalties: 8
Va'a 8
Leading point scorers:
49 Va'a
15 Lima
10 Fa'asavalu, Sititi, Palepoi, Feaunati, Tagicakibau

SCOTLAND
Matches: 5
Won: 3
Lost: 2
Pool result: 2nd 14 points
Eliminated in quarter-final (Australia)
Points for: 118
Points against: 130
Tries: 12
Paterson 3, Danielli 3, Grimes, Taylor, Kerr, Townsend, Smith, Russell
Conversions: 8
Paterson 7, Townsend
Penalties: 13
Paterson 12, Townsend
Drop goals: 1
Paterson
Leading point scorers:
68 Paterson
15 Danielli
10 Townsend

FRANCE

Matches: 7
Won: 5
Lost: 2
Pool result: 1st, 20 points
Eliminated in semi-final (England); lost playoff to New Zealand and finished fourth
Points for: 267
Points against: 155
Tries: 29
Dominici 4, Jauzion 3, Harinordoquy 3, Liebenberg 3, Rougerie 2, Michalak 2, Crenca 2, Betsen 2, Ibanez, Pelous, Galthie, Brusque, Bru, Poux, Magne, Elhorga
Conversions: 22
Michalak 18, Merceron 3, Yachvili
Penalties: 22
Michalak 18, Merceron 3, Yachvili 1
Drop goals: 4
Yachvili 2, Michalak, Brusque
Leading point scorers:
103 Michalak
20 Dominici

GEORGIA

Matches: 4
Won: 0
Lost: 4
Pool result: 5th 0 points
Points for: 46
Points against: 200
Tries: 1
Dadunashvili
Conversions: 1
Jimsheladze
Penalties: 12
Jimsheladze 6, Kvirikashvili 4, Urjukashvili 2
Drop goals: 1
Jimsheladze
Leading point scorers:
23 Jimsheladze
12 Kvirikashvili

IRELAND

Matches: 5
Won: 3
Lost: 2
Pool result: 2nd 15 points
Eliminated in quarter-final (France)
Points for: 162
Points against: 99
Tries: 20
O'Driscoll 3, Hickie 3, Quinlan 3, Miller 2, S. Horgan 2, Wood, Costello, Dempsey, Horan, G. Easterby, Maggs, Kelly
Conversions: 16
O'Gara 9, Humphreys 7
Penalties: 9
Humphreys 5, O'Gara 4
Drop goals: 1
O'Driscoll
Leading point scorers:
30 O'Gara
29 Humphreys
18 O'Driscoll

ITALY

Matches: 4
Won: 1
Lost: 3
Pool result: 3rd 8 points
Points for: 77
Points against: 123
Tries: 5
D. Dallan 2, M. Dallan, Phillips, Parisse
Conversions: 5
Wakarua 4, Peens
Penalties: 14
Wakarua 14
Leading point scorers:
50 Wakarua
10 D. Dallan

JAPAN

Matches: 4
Won: 0
Lost: 4
Pool result: 5th 0 points
Points for: 79
Points against: 163
Tries: 6
Ohata 2, Onasawa, Konia, Miller, Kurihara
Conversions: 5
Kurihara 4, Miller
Penalties: 12
Kurihara 9, Hirose 2, Miller
Drop goals: 1
Miller
Leading point scorers:
40 Kurihara
13 Miller
10 Ohata

SOUTH AFRICA

Matches: 5
Won: 3
Lost: 2
Pool result: 2nd 14 points
Eliminated in quarter-final (New Zealand)
Points for: 193
Points against: 63
Tries: 27
Van der Westhuizen 3, van Niekerk 3, Botha 3, Fourie 3, Rossouw 3, Hougaard 2, Delport, Bands, Scholtz, Greeff, Burger, Muller, Smith, van der Westhuyzen, de Kock, Willemse
Conversions: 17
Hougaard 10, Koen 7
Penalties: 7
Hougaard 5, Koen 2
Drop goals: 1
Hougaard
Leading point scorers:
48 Hougaard
20 Koen
15 Van der Westhuizen, van Niekerk, Botha, Fourie, Rossouw

TONGA

Matches: 4
Won: 0
Lost: 4
Pool result: 5th 1 point
Points for: 46
Points against: 178
Tries: 7
Hola 2, Payne, Tu'ifua, Kivalu, Lavaka, Afeaki
Conversions: 4
Tu'ipolotu 2, Hola 2
Penalties: 1
Hola
Leading point scorers:
17 Hola

URUGUAY

Matches: 4
Won: 1
Lost: 3
Pool result: 4th 4 points
Points for: 56
Points against: 255
Tries: 6
Lemoine 2, Capo, Cardoso, Lamelas, Brignoni
Conversions: 4
Aguirre 2, Menchaca 2
Penalties: 6
Aguirre 3, Menchaca 3
Leading point scorers:
13 Aguirre, Menchaca
10 Lemoine

USA

Matches: 4
Won: 1
Lost: 3
Pool result: 4th 6 points
Points for: 86
Points against: 125
Tries: 9
Schubert 3, Van Zyl 2, Hercus 2, Eloff, Khasigian
Conversions: 7
Hercus 7
Penalties: 9
Hercus 9
Leading point scorers:
51 Hercus
15 Schubert
10 Van Zyl

WALES

Matches: 5
Won: 3
Lost: 2
Pool result: 2nd 14 points
Eliminated in quarter-final (England)
Points for: 149
Points against: 126
Tries: 17
M. Williams 3, Charvis 3, Parker 3, M. Jones 2, Cooper 2, D. Jones, S. Jones, G. Thomas, Taylor
Conversions: 14
Harris 9, S. Jones 5
Penalties: 11
S. Jones 7, Harris 4
Drop goals: 1
M. Williams
Leading point scorers:
36 S. Jones
30 Harris
18 M. Williams

Leading scorers at Rugby World Cup 2003

POINTS

113	**JONNY WILKINSON**	England
103	**FREDERIC MICHALAK**	France
100	**ELTON FLATLEY**	Australia
75	**LEON MACDONALD**	New Zealand
68	**CHRIS PATERSON**	Scotland
57	**MAT ROGERS**	Australia
51	**MIKE HERCUS**	USA
50	**RIMA WAKARUA**	Italy
49	**EARL VA'A**	Samoa

TRIES

7	**DOUG HOWLETT**	New Zealand
7	**MILS MULIAINA**	New Zealand
6	**JOE ROKOCOKO**	New Zealand
5	**WILL GREENWOOD**	England
5	**CHRIS LATHAM**	Australia
5	**JOSH LEWSEY**	England
5	**MAT ROGERS**	Australia
5	**LOTE TUQIRI**	Australia

CONVERSIONS

20	**LEON MACDONALD**	New Zealand
19	**DANIEL CARTER**	New Zealand
18	**FREDERIC MICHALAK**	France
16	**ELTON FLATLEY**	Australia
16	**MAT ROGERS**	Australia
15	**PAUL GRAYSON**	England
10	**DERICK HOUGAARD**	South Africa
10	**JONNY WILKINSON**	England
10	**EARL VA'A**	Samoa

PENALTIES

23	**JONNY WILKINSON**	England
21	**ELTON FLATLEY**	Australia
18	**FREDERIC MICHALAK**	France
14	**RIMA WAKARUA**	Italy
12	**CHRIS PATERSON**	Scotland
11	**NICKY LITTLE**	Fiji
9	**TORU KURIHARA**	Japan
9	**MIKE HERCUS**	USA
8	**EARL VA'A**	Samoa
7	**STEPHEN JONES**	Wales

DROP GOALS

8	**JONNY WILKINSON**	England
2	**DMITRI YACHVILI**	France

Across the 48 matches at RWC 2003:

- 180 players scored tries
- 40 players converted tries
- 35 players kicked penalties
- 15 players dropped goals

Team tournament totals

	TEAM	POINTS	TRIES	CONVERSIONS	PENALTIES	DROP GOALS
1.	NEW ZEALAND	361	52	40	6	1
2.	AUSTRALIA	345	43	32	21	1
3.	ENGLAND	327	36	27	23	8
4.	FRANCE	267	29	22	22	4
5.	SOUTH AFRICA	193	27	17	7	1
6.	IRELAND	162	20	16	9	1
7.	WALES	149	17	14	11	1
8.	ARGENTINA	140	18	13	6	2
9.	SAMOA	138	18	12	8	-
10.	SCOTLAND	118	12	8	13	1
11.	FIJI	98	10	6	12	-
12.	USA	86	9	7	9	-
13.	JAPAN	79	6	5	12	1
14.	ITALY	77	5	5	14	-
15.	ROMANIA	65	8	5	5	-
16.	URUGUAY	56	6	4	6	-
17.	CANADA	54	4	2	9	1
18.	TONGA	46	7	4	1	-
19.	GEORGIA	46	1	1	12	1
20.	NAMIBIA	28	4	4	-	-

A photographer captures the emotion of the crowd after England's semi-final victory over France in Sydney.

Travelling north: For the first time, a Northern Hemisphere nation has taken possession of the Webb Ellis Cup. English coach Clive Woodward gives the Australian public one last look at the trophy before his team takes it to England, where it will reside until RWC 2007 in France.